Contents

Part 1

The Russian Empire

1 Travelling in the Russian Empire

In the 1870s a Scotsman, Mackenzie Wallace, visited many parts of the Russian Empire. These passages from his book, Russia, *describe different ways of travelling about the huge land. All the places mentioned can be found in Source 2C. Notice that Wallace calls the people of the River Don district 'Cossacks'. They were the descendants of people who had set up frontier settlements there two centuries before.*

A By train

The carriages are decidedly better than in England, and in winter they are kept warm by small iron stoves, assisted by double windows and double doors – a very necessary precaution in a land where the thermometer often falls to 30 degrees below zero. The trains never attain. it is true, a high rate of speed – so at least English and Americans think – but then we must remember that Russians are rarely in a hurry, and like to have frequent opportunities of eating and drinking. . . . From Moscow to St. Petersburg the locomotive runs for a distance of 400 miles [643 kilometres] almost as the crow is supposed to fly, turning to neither the right hand nor to the left. For twelve weary hours the passenger in the express train looks out on forest and morass*, and rarely catches sight of human habitation.

From D. Mackenzie Wallace. *Russia,* Cassell & Co., 2nd edn. 1912.

* *area of marshy ground.*

B By boat, on the river Don

The river is extremely shallow, and the sandbanks are continually shifting, so that many times in the course of the day the steamer runs aground. Sometimes she is got off by simply reversing the engines. . . . The captain always gave a number of stalwart Cossacks* a free passage on condition that they should give him the assistance he required; and as soon as the ship stuck fast, he ordered them to jump overboard with a stout hawser* and pull them off.

From D. Mackenzie Wallace. *Russia,* Cassell & Co., 2nd edn. 1912.

* *people of the Don region*

* *thick rope or wire*

C Travelling by Imperial post service

One has to apply to the proper authorities for a . . . large sheet of paper stamped with the Imperial Eagle, and bearing the name of the recipient, the destination and the number of horses to be supplied.

. . . Armed with this document you go to the post-station and demand the requisite number of horses. The vehicle . . . resembles an enormous cradle on wheels. . . . An armful of hay spread over the bottom of the wooden box is supposed to play the part of seats and cushions.

From D. Mackenzie Wallace. *Russia*, Cassell & Co., 2nd edn. 1912.

D Crossing a bridge

Making hurriedly the sign of the cross, he gathers up his reins, waves his little whip in the air, and, shouting lustily, urges on his team. . . . First there is a short descent; then the horses plunge wildly through a zone of deep mud; next comes a fearful jolt, as the vehicle is jerked up on to the first planks; then the tranverse planks . . . rattle and rumble ominously at the . . . animals pick their way cautiously and gingerly among the dangerous holes and crevices; lastly you plunge with a horrible jolt into a second mud zone.

From D. Mackenzie Wallace. *Russia*, Cassell & Co., 2nd edn. 1912.

Questions

1 How did travelling by train in Russia differ from travelling by train in England?

2 What was the main problem of travelling by boat?

3 What obstacles did the Russian government put in the way of those travellers wanting to use the Imperial post service?

4 Which method of travelling through Russia would you have preferred? Give reasons for your answer.

5 Can you suggest why the Moscow–St Petersburg railway ran in an almost straight line?

2 The Russian Empire before 1914

Before 1914 only about half the Empire's people were Great Russians; those who spoke the Russian language. In the west the Empire included much of modern Finland and Poland as well as areas which were the homes of Ukrainians, Lithuanians, Latvians and many others. In the south, there were many conquered Asiatic people such as Kazakhs and Kirgiz. The Cossacks lived in the steppes; especially around the lower banks of the rivers Don, Dnieper and Volga.

A The steppes *A drawing (by C. Bossili) of the steppes, showing a party of nomads or traders on the move. Houses in this treeless area are usually made of mud bricks.*

B The taiga *The taiga or pine forest, which is snow-covered from November to March. Wooden houses were built in scattered clearings. The photograph was taken in 1880.*

C The Russian Empire before 1914

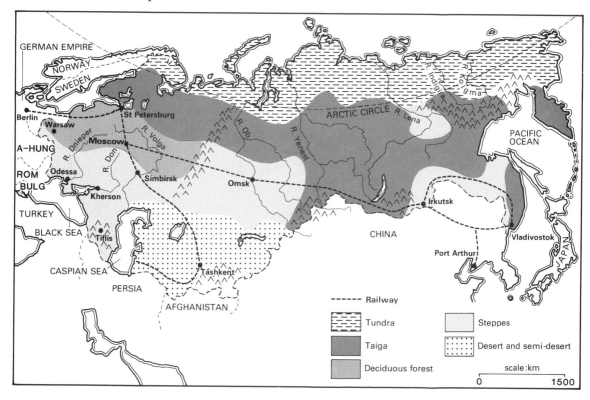

Questions

Use Source 1 and the photograph on page 9 to help you answer these questions.

1 How might you have travelled from Moscow to St Petersburg? How long would the journey have taken?

2 What might have been the best way of travelling from Moscow to the Caspian Sea?

3 How long would it have taken to travel by rail from St Petersburg to Vladivostok?

4 Describe the changes in the countryside that you would see on a rail journey from St Petersburg to Tashkent.

5 Supposing your great grandfather had taken a job as a merchant in China in 1910. How would he have got there most quickly?

6 Which of the Empire's frontiers do you think would have been most difficult to defend?

7 Which different forms of transport for men and goods can you see in the photographs?

8 What sort of vegetation would you find on the taiga and the steppes?

3 Peasants' homes

There were 129 million people counted in the Russian census of 1897. Most of them were poor peasants living in tiny wooden homes which straggled along both sides of a muddy or dusty village street. The peasants farmed strips of land in the fields around. This is an Englishman's description of the inside of a peasant family's home, published in 1913. It refers to the 'black earth' district around the upper Volga which was the most fertile part of the flat grasslands known as the steppes.

A A peasant family's home

Wooden benches stand along the walls, also a construction of planks on which the inmates make their beds. In some districts there is a bedstead used by the peasant and his wife. At the entrance there are black pictures of saints whose features are no longer recognizable, ancient heirlooms held in high honour; even in very poor houses a little lamp is kept burning night and day before them. The table utensils are kept in a cupboard, which finishes the furniture of the rom, for the Russian peasant knows no chairs. When he comes home in the winter stiff and covered with snow, he takes off his shoes and stretches himself out by the stove. . . .

A small hut about twelve feet [3.6 metres] square – with a door through which a medium-sized man can only go by stooping – the floor made of earth, the ceiling so low that a tall man cannot stand upright, tiny windows letting in but little light with much draught and cold – the whole building made of thin wood, insufficiently plugged with oakum*. That is the usual peasant's home in Russia! and these poor peasants constitute nine-tenths of the population.

The stove takes up a quarter of the room, that is, the particular Russian stove. It heats the room and cooks the food, it bakes the bread and boils the dirty clothes, and all the members of the family bathe in it in turns, and the old people sleep on it. It is the universal stove which only a people under snow six months out of every year could have invented. And what do they not use to heat it – wood, straw, dung. . . .

It is torture to go into a peasant's hut when the stove is being lit. The room is full of smoke, no one can breathe, it is suffocating; the smoke stings the eyes, that is why there are so many blind people in Russia. The real Russian stove has no chimney. The smoke fills the room and tries to escape through the roof, through the thatch, or the holes in the walls – and when the peasant can stand the accumulated smoke no longer, through the open door. . . .

From D. S. Rappoport,
Home Life in Russia,
Methuen, 1913.

strands of rope, usually waxed or tarred, which were used to plug cracks.

The entire family live in this room, day and night. The old man mends his shoes and the women work the spinning-wheel; the girls and young children sit here; the babe cries in his cradle; a calf, a lamb, a sucking-pig huddle together round the stove – here they are warm, and if left in the outhouses would freeze to death. They sleep on the benches and on the floor all together, men, women, old men, children, and cattle.

Questions

1 What can you learn from this description about the climate in this part of Russia?

2 Why were the pictures of the saints black?

3 What was the most important piece of furniture or equipment in a peasant's hut? Why was this so?

4 In what ways would your life be different from now if you lived in this home?

5 How does the size of this hut compare with the largest room in your home?

6 Use the photographs on pages 4 and 9 to describe homes in three different parts of the Empire.

4 A famine, 1892

There was hardly any year when the crops did not fail in some part of the Empire. If the grain was destroyed by disease or bad weather the result was a dreadful famine the following winter. These accounts were written by a Russian lady who led a relief party which took food to villages in the Volga river area, which were suffering famine in 1892.

A Hunger in the villages

It was a tragedy to see splendid men in the prime of their life walking about with stony faces and hollow eyes. And then there were women clothed only in wretched rags, and little children shivering in the cold wind. They would crowd around the relief parties, which drove about in sledges, holding out their hands saying:

> We have sold our last horses, cows and sheep, we have pawned all our winter clothing: we have nothing left to sell. We eat but once a day, stewed cabbage and stewed pumpkins and many of us have not eaten that.

This was true. There were many among them who had not tasted food for days. It was agonising to hear these poor people pleading to us for mercy lest they die of starvation. As they spoke in dull voices, tears would spring up out of the eyes of strong men and course slowly down their cheeks into their rough beards; but there was no complaint, no cries, just the slow monotonous chant, broken by the sobs of worn out mothers and the cries of hungry children.

The thermometer stood at 36°F. below freezing point, yet the air was so calm that the cold was scarcely noticeable.

From O. Novikoff, Russian Memories, H. Jenkins Ltd, 1916.

B A family's suffering

Paul Axenoff is the head of a family of nine, two old people, Axenoff and his wife, and five children.... The house and cow have been sold and the outhouses pulled down and used for fuel. Straw is usually employed in Russia for heating, but this year there is none, so the peasants are glad to find anything to burn. ... In this hut I discovered a fresh article of food – a soup made of hot water and weeds. They didn't eat it for the good it might do them, but simply for the sake of having something hot. At another hut in this village I found a similar concoction made with boiling water and chopped-up hay.

From O. Novikoff, Russian Memories, H. Jenkins Ltd, 1916.

C Starving peasants

A photograph taken in the Volga region during the famine of 1892. Starving peasants are being given soup.

Questions

1 What do you find the most distressing part of the descriptions in Sources A and B?

2 Supposing Paul Axenoff's family did not die during the famine, what problems would they have in 1893?

3 Other parts of Russia did not have a famine in 1892. Can you suggest reasons why these villagers were so short of food?

4 Can you see any evidence that the photograph was taken in the district described by the writer? Does it show the same time of year?

5 A day in the life of a landowner

Near to most villages was the home and fields of a nobleman. Until 1861 the peasants had been his serfs. This meant the nobleman had the right to sell them, to make them work on his lands, to punish them by ordering whippings. Now they were free men but many still worked on his lands as labourers and the government still expected noblemen to supervise the affairs of village communities. Yet most country noblemen left it to their stewards to manage their farms and lived lives very similar to that of Ivan Ivanovitch, here described by Mackenzie Wallace, the traveller who wrote Source 1.

A Ivan Ivanovitch's day

Ivan Ivanovitch gets up about seven o'clock, and puts on, with the assistance of his valet-de-chambre, a simple costume consisting chiefly of a faded, plentifully stained dressing gown. Having nothing in particular to do, he sits down at the open window and looks into the yard. . . . Towards nine o'clock tea is announced, and he goes into the dining room. . . . As this morning meal consists merely of bread and tea, it does not last long; and all disperse to their several occupations. The head of the house begins the labours of the day by resuming his seat at the open window. . . . Here he sits tranquilly till the sun has so far moved round that the verandah at the back of the house is completely in the shade, when he has his arm-chair removed thither, and sits there till dinner-time. . . .

Dinner is the great event of the day. The food is abundant and of good quality, but mushrooms, onions, and fat play a rather too important part. . . . No sooner has the last dish been removed than a death-like stillness falls upon the house: it is the time of the afternoon siesta. . . .

In about two hours the house gradually re-wakens. . . . Soon a man-servant issues from the kitchen bearing an enormous tea-urn, which puffs like a little steam engine. . . .

In the evening it often happens that a little group of peasants come into the court, and ask to see the 'master' . . . Stepping forward a little, and bowing low, one of the group begins. . . 'Little Father, Ivan Ivanovitch, be gracious; you are the father, and we are your children' – and so on . . . till at last his patience is exhausted and he says to them in a paternal tone, 'Now enough! you are blockheads'. . . .

A regular part of the evening's occupation is the interview with the steward. The work that has just been done, and the programme for the morrow, are always discussed at great length . . . till supper is announced, and immediately after that meal . . . all retire for the night.

From D. Mackenzie Wallace, *Russia*, Cassell & Co., 2nd edn. 1912.

B The nobleman's residence

A photograph of a nobleman's house, built in the eighteenth century.

Questions

1 How would you have felt if you were the teenage son or daughter of Ivan Ivanovitch?

2 Would you describe Ivan as a good landlord?

3 Can you explain why the peasants treated him so respectfully despite his bad temper towards them?

4 What was the job of a valet-de-chambre?

5 What does the photograph tell you about the nobleman's way of life? How was it different from the lives of the peasants whose homes are shown on page 9?

6 The civil service

The head of the Russian state was the Tsar or Emperor. Tsar Peter the Great (1681–1725) had set up a complicated civil service to carry out the government. By 1900 it had tens of thousands of officials. At the top were the ministers in charge of the various government departments in St Petersburg. At the bottom were customs officials and post office workers. The Empire was divided into provinces or 'governments', headed by a governor, which were broken up into districts. These districts were divided into rural areas, where a 'Warden of the Peasantry' looked after the affairs of several villages. Everything that was done by civil servants in these local positions had to be approved in St Petersburg. The following passage is taken from a book written in 1915 by an American who had made a careful study of Russia.

A The civil service in action

A Russian may wear uniform his whole life long. As a little boy of eight he goes proudly off to a preparatory school in a long grey overcoat, reaching almost to the ground, and in a broad-crowned cap with the peak tilted over his snub nose. When school days are over he dons the uniform of a student, and after a few years at University or Technical College, enters a Ministry and puts on one of the many official uniforms. The years pass, he is gradually promoted, and at fifty he is trudging in uniform with portfolio under his arm to his Ministry, just as with bag on shoulders he tramped to school when he was a little boy of eight.

From H. Williams, *Russia of the Russians*, Charles Scribner's Sons (NY), 1915.

All the Government officials are Chinovniks, that is to say, each of them stands in a definite *chin*, or rank. Peter the Great established an order of promotion called the *Tabel Rangov*, or Table of Ranks, and this order is in force to the present day. Once a man is drawn into the subtle mechanism of the Table of Ranks he may go on from grade to grade with hardly an effort on his part, by the mere fact of existing and growing wrinkled and grey-haired.

From the big dreary-looking yellow or brown buildings in St. Petersburg, in which the ministries are housed, currents of authority, or directive energy go forth to all the ends of the great Empire in the form of telegrams or occasional oral messages by special couriers, but above all in the form of endless 'papers'. Pens scratch, typewriters click, clerks lay blue covers full of papers before the 'head of the table', 'the head of the table' sends them to the head of the department, to the Assistant Minister, if need be, and in the more important cases, the Assistant Minister to the Minister. Then back go the papers again with signatures appended, down through various grades for despatch to a judge, to another department, to a Governor, to a *chinovnik* on special service, or to some petitioner from the world without.

All sorts of documents go under the general name of *bumaga* or 'paper' from a warrant for arrest to a report on a projected railway, or a notification of taxes due. . . . Authority is delegated from the big yellow ministries in St. Petersburg to the dreary white towns of the governments or territories into which the whole Empire is mapped out, and from the government towns to the head towns of the districts into which each government is divided, and then down to the smallest towns and to the Wardens of the Peasantry.

Questions

1 Describe the civil service of the Russian Empire in your own words.

2 Imagine you lived in a village near Omsk and a bridge needed repairing. Who would you first report to? What might happen next to your report? Who might finally decide what to do?

3 Why were government officials known as *chinovniks*?

4 From a present day point of view can you think of any disadvantages in the Russian Empire's civil service?

7 The Church

Most of the Russians in the Empire belonged to the Russian Orthodox Church. The organisation of the Church was controlled by the government which expected priests to teach loyalty to the Tsar. This was one reason why village people had little respect for the priests; another was that they had to pay him fees at different times. Most peasants probably understood little of the religious services they attended, but they looked forward to feast days.

In the first passage a parish priest is complaining to a Scotsman, Mackenzie Wallace, who toured Russia in the 1870s. In the second, Mackenzie Wallace describes a feast-day and a religious procession. Here priests carried ikons, which are pictures of saints made partly of enamel paint and partly of silver. Two men carried a bier, or stretcher, holding a silver ark which contained religious scrolls.

A The village priest

'Perhaps you have heard that the parish priest extorts money from the peasants – refusing to perform the rites of baptism or burial until a considerable sum has been paid. It is only too true, but who is to blame? The priest must live and bring up his family. . . . When I make the periodical visitation I can see that the peasants grudge every handful of rye and every egg that they give me. I can overhear their sneers as I go away, and I know they have many sayings such as, "The priest takes from the living and from the dead." Many of them fasten their doors, pretending to be away from home, and do not even take the precaution of keeping silent till I am out of hearing.'

'You surprise me,' I said, 'I have always heard that the Russians are a very religious people – at least, the lower classes.'

'So they are; but the peasantry are poor and heavily taxed. They set great importance on the sacraments, and observe rigorously the fasts, which comprise nearly a half of the year; but they show very little respect for their priests, who are almost as poor as themselves.'

From D. Mackenzie Wallace, *Russia*, Cassell & Co., 2nd edn. 1912.

B A Church feastday in Moscow

It is a mass of colour; red, black, cream, yellow, blue, and lilac. All the men are bareheaded; there is plenty of interest, but no pushing. Soldiers and police keep open a passage, along which pass little bands of priests in full vestments, and Church officials, carrying the ikons, banners and crosses of their parishes. Suddenly from the high belfry there rings out first one little bell, then the great ones; the quick peal of all the little bells joins in. An awe comes over the multitude; all cross themselves devoutly. . . . The slow procession sways forward, first sixty Church banners, with tassels yellow, orange, or red, then on one side fifty priests bearing crosses, and on the other the Church officials carrying the dark ikons in their gorgeous frames. And now passes the silver ark,

From D. Mackenzie Wallace, *Russia*, Cassell & Co., 2nd edn. 1912.

borne on high; all along the road the peasants throw on to the bier little squares of coarse cloth, which they have worked as offerings, and which are later sold for the profit of the Cathedral.

The peasants sit down anywhere on the grass in family groups, all simple and good-humoured. The procession has broken up, and each little group of priests and ikons makes its way back to its own parish. As long as their direction permits, groups still march together. Many stay the evening on the great waste patch by the river, where stalls have been set up. There one can buy very sugary biscuits, simple quaint toys, or clothes. A peasant runs along holding out his jacket. 'Who'll buy this? I must have money for beer.'

C A Russian church

Inside a Russian Orthodox church. Notice the Greek, or Byzantine, style of architecture and the elaborate dress of the priests taking part in a religious procession.

Questions

1 How does the priest explain the peasants' dislike of priests?

2 How does he defend priests?

3 From the evidence in these two extracts, in what ways do the Russians appear to be a religious people?

4 Use the picture to add to Mackenzie Wallace's information about the vestments worn by the priests and the banners and crosses they carried.

5 In what ways does the architecture of an orthodox church differ from that of most churches in Britain?

6 Suggest a reason why the ikons are said to be 'dark'.

8 St Petersburg workers

Until the middle of the nineteenth century St Petersburg was a city of elegant government buildings, cathedrals and the homes of the rich. By 1900, only fifty years later, it contained about a million factory workers and their families, most of them living in crowded slums to the north of the city centre. Father Gapon was a priest who sympathised with the hard life of these people. Here he is writing about cotton workers.

A The life of cotton workers

They receive miserable wages, and generally live in an overcrowded state, very commonly in special lodging houses. A woman takes several rooms in her own name, subletting each one; and it is common to see ten or even more persons living in one room and four sleeping in one bed.

The normal working day . . . is eleven and a half hours of work, exclusive of meal times. But . . . manufacturers have received permission to work overtime, so that the average day is longer than nominally allowed by law – fourteen or fifteen hours. I often watched the crowds of poorly clad and emaciated figures of men and girls returning from the mills. It was a heartrending sight. The grey faces seemed dead, or relieved only by eyes blazing with the rage of desperate revolt. Why do they agree to work overtime? They have to do so because they are paid by the piece and the rate is very low. Returning home exhausted and resentful after his long day's labour, the workman sees the sad faces of his wife and hungry children in their squalid corner where they are packed like herrings. What wonder that . . . he carries some of his small earnings to the public house and spends them on vodkha! If he does not become a habitual drunkard, it must often be because he has not the money.

For fifteen and twenty years, and often less, of such a life, even if they have not succumbed to accident or illness, men and women lose altogether their vitality and capacity for strenuous labour. Then they lose their places in the mill. Crowds of such unemployed are to be seen at the factory gates in the early morning. There they stand and wait until the foreman comes out to engage a few, if there be any vacant places. Badly clad and underfed, waiting in the terrible frosty mornings of the St. Petersburg winter, they present a sight that makes one shudder.

From G. Gapon, *The Story of my Life*, Chapman & Hall, 1905.

B Living conditions

Tenants in one of the flats in a poor area of St Petersburg. The photograph was taken in the late 1890s.

Questions

1 Why did factory workers labour for such long hours?

2 According to Father Gapon what causes a man to turn to drink?

3 What reason does he give for men losing their places in the mill?

4 Can you link Father Gapon's description with any period in British history?

5 Does the photograph give any further evidence about the lives of factory workers? What do you think is the purpose of the material hanging in the room?

6 Compare these sources with Sources 3 and 4 on life in the countryside. In which ways was a town worker's life better and in which ways was it worse than a peasant's? You might think about this under headings such as housing, food, hours and conditions of work.

9 'Bloody Sunday' 1905

In the winter of 1904–5 conditions for working people in St Petersburg became even worse than before. This was mainly because the Russian Empire was at war with Japan and food supplies to the city had broken down, while many factories had stopped working because of the shortage of materials.

In January 1905 hundreds of workers and their families, led by Father Gapon who wrote the description of factory workers in Source 8, marched to the Tsar's Winter Palace with a letter. The letter asked the Tsar for better conditions and a say in the government. Source A gives part of the letter; Source B is a description of what happened, written by Alexander Kerensky who later become Prime Minister. You can find the Nevsky Prospect and the Winter Palace on the map on page 34.

A   The petition to the Tsar

Oh Sire, we working men of St. Petersburg, our wives and children and our parents, helpless and aged women and men, have come to you, our ruler, in search of justice and protection. We are beggars, we are oppressed and overburdened with work; we are insulted, we are not looked on as humans beings but are treated as slaves.

B   The fate of the marchers

Along the Nevsky Prospect from the direction of the working-class districts came row upon row of orderly and solemn faced workers all dressed in their best clothes. Gapon, marching in front of the procession was carrying a cross, and a number of the workers were holding icons and portraits of the Tsar. . . .

We had already reached the Alexander Garden, on the other side of which lay the Winter Palace Square, when we heard the sound of bugles, the signal for the cavalry to charge. The marchers came to a halt, uncertain as to what the bugles meant and unable to see what was happening. In front, on the right, was a detachment of police, but since they showed no signs of hostility, the procession began moving again. Just then, however, a detachment of cavalry rode out. . . . The first volley was fired in the air, but the second was aimed at the crowd, and a number of people fell to the ground. Panic-stricken, the crowd turned and began running in every direction. They were now being fired on from behind, and we bystanders took to our heels with the rest. I cannot describe the horror I felt at that moment. It was quite clear the authorities had made

From A. Kerensky, *Russia and History's Turning Point*, Orwell, Shaw & Pearce (NY), 1965

a terrible mistake; they had totally misunderstood the intentions of the crowd. Whatever the plans of the organisers of the march may have been, the workers went to the palace without any evil intent. They sincerely believed that when they got there they would kneel down and the Tsar would come out to meet them or at least appear on the balcony. But all they got was bullets.

The first estimates showed the number of casualties to be at least two or three hundred killed and wounded. Ambulances were quickly called and those who had not been hurt helped to carry the wounded men, women and children. Everything broke in confusion, and the crowd eventually dispersed into the neighbouring streets. . . .

Questions

1 Why do you think the day has become known as 'Bloody Sunday'?

2 What phrases and words in Source A suggest that the marchers were loyal subjects of the Tsar?

3 Is there any evidence in the extracts to suggest that the workers were in a violent mood?

4 From your reading of Source B do you think the troops wanted to clear the demonstration or to injure the marchers?

5 Do you think 'Bloody Sunday' might have made any difference in working people's attitudes towards the Tsar?

6 What does the second extract tell you about Alexander Kerensky's political sympathies?

7 Imagine you had been one of the marchers. Write notes for a political speech you would make to a meeting of working men a few days after 'Bloody Sunday'.

10 A pogrom, 1905

The non-Russian people in the Empire were continually persecuted. Their position became worse when the Tsar and his ministers tried to turn opposition from themselves towards the minority peoples. They encouraged Russians to believe that the non-Russian people were to blame for social problems or defeats in war.

After the Empire was beaten by Japan in the war of 1904–5 the five million Jews who lived in western Russia became the victims of brutal raids or pogroms. The government ordered that the police should not interfere with pogroms carried out by the Union of the Russian people, a right-wing organisation which set out to terrorise any groups they thought were not totally loyal to the Tsar.

These accounts tell how a landowning family found that their head watchman was taking part in pogroms. Because the police would not act, the writer and his father themselves went to save a Jew living on their land. The photograph shows the results from an even more brutal pogrom.

A Taking part in pogroms

One day our head watchman Yegor suddenly disappeared, returning after a few days with a large stock of jewellery. Then we learned – Yegor himself made no attempt to keep the matter secret – that the most ghastly Jewish pogroms had taken place in Kieff in which he too had taken part, as he eventually told us with undisguised glee. After his return he collected a gang to go and rob our tenant Girsha Kaplan. As soon as my mother discovered the intention she sent off a mounted messenger asking to have Yegor arrested, more especially as Yegor himself had admitted the part he had played in the Kieff pogroms. Hereupon the local authority replied to my mother that not only was Yegor's arrest impossible in consequence of the order given by a higher authority that members of the 'Union of the Russian People' were not to be arrested . . . but that they were as far as possible not to interfere in Jew pogroms. . . .

From V. Kovostovetz, Seed and Harvest, Faber & Faber, 1931.

B Attempts to halt a pogrom

From afar we heard a wild confusion of voices coming from the village where the meeting was taking place. As we approached, we saw youths armed with clubs and axes hammering in Girsha's gate. They broke in and got hold of the praying Girsha, for it was the Sabbath, and dragged him into the village street clothed in his praying garments. There they thrashed him before the eyes of his old wife and his children. The children were not neglected either. Pillows and beds were flung out of the windows; peasant women were quarrelling over them and dragging them off home, while some boy kept yelling through it all: 'The Jews are being thrashed – the Jews are being thrashed,' while he danced about with old Girsha's huge tall hat on his head.

From V. Kovostovetz, Seed and Harvest, Faber & Faber, 1931.

In supreme command of all this was Yegor, who had clutched the old Jew by the beard and by threatening him with a dagger, was trying to make him say where he had hidden his money. When Yegor saw us he quite lost his head; and he had cause to. On our horses we dashed in among the crowd, scattering them with our whips. Then the puzzled peasants, scratching their heads in doubt, began to murmur: 'What the devil . . . here we are told that the Tsar ordered us to plunder the Jews, because it's all their fault the way the war has ended . . . and now the gentry come thrashing round with nagaikas!'* They hung about for a while and then went home.

Russian for whip

C   The results of a pogrom

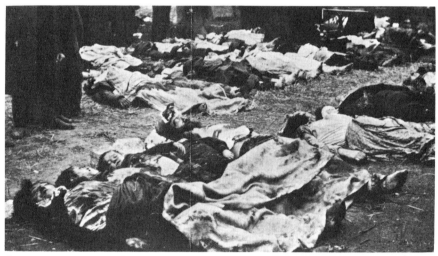

Jews awaiting burial after a pogrom in 1905. The events here were obviously more brutal than those described in the document.

Questions

1 Can you explain the behaviour of Yegor?

2 Why would the local authority not arrest Yegor?

3 Why were the peasants puzzled when they were stopped from attacking the Jews?

4 Try to imagine that you had been present at the events described. What would your feelings have been as a teenage Russian peasant of the time?

5 What does the photograph tell you about the victims of a pogrom? Which aspects of the scene has the photographer focused on?

11 Exiled to Siberia

At the age of eighteen, along with other young men and women, Lev Bronstein was secretly printing a magazine to spread socialist ideas among workers in south Russia. At nineteen he was arrested and held for two years in three different prisons before being sent into exile, banished, to Siberia. Bronstein was a political prisoner, not a criminal, so in all this time he did not have a trial.

Bronstein later took the name Trotsky and became an important revolutionary leader. In this passage from his own life story he describes the journey to Siberia and his exile with his wife. You can find the river Lena on the map on page 5.

A Life in Siberia

We were going down the river Lena, a few barges of convicts, with a convoy of soldiers, drifting slowly along with the current. It was cold at night, and the heavy coats with which we covered ourselves were thick with frost in the morning. All along the way, at villages decided on beforehand, one or two convicts were put ashore. As well as I can remember it took about three weeks before we came to the village of Ust-Kut. There I was put ashore with one of the women prisoners, a close associate of mine from Nikolayev. Alexandra Lvovna had one of the important positions in the South Russian Workers' Union. . . . The work that were doing bound us closely together, and so, to avoid being separated, we had been married in the transfer prison in Moscow.

The village comprised about a hundred peasant huts. We settled down in one of them, on the very edge of the village. About us were the woods; below us, the river. Farther north, down the Lena, there were gold-mines. The reflection of the gold seemed to hover about the river. . . .

In the summer our lives were made wretched by midges. They even bit to death a cow which had lost its way in the woods. The peasants wore nets of tarred horsehair over their heads. In the spring and autumn the village was buried in mud. To be sure, the country was beautiful, but during these years it left me cold. I hated to waste interest and time on it. I lived between the woods and the river, and I hardly noticed them – I was so busy with my books and personal relations. I was studying Marx, brushing the cockroaches off the page.

The Lena was the great water route of the exiled. Those who had completed their terms returned to the south by way of the river. But communication was continuous between these various nests of the banished which kept growing with the rise of the revolutionary tide. The exiles exchanged letters with each other. . . .

From L. Trotsky, *My Life*, Butterworth, 1930.

The exiles were no longer willing to stay in their places of confinement, and there was an epidemic of escapes. We had to arrange a system of rotation. In almost every village there were individual peasants who as youths had come under the influence of the older revolutionaries. They would carry the 'politicals' away secretly in boats, in carts or in sledges, and pass them along from one to another. The police in Siberia were as helpless as we were. The vastness of the country was an ally, but an enemy as well. It was very hard to catch a runaway, but the chances were that he would be drowned in the river or frozen to death in the primeval forests.

Questions

1 What does Trotsky tell you about the climate and way of life in Siberia?

2 What reason does Trotsky give for having married Alexandra Lvovna?

3 How did Trotsky spend his time in exile? Does this tell you anything about the kind of man he was?

4 What was 'the revolutionary tide' Trotsky speaks of?

5 Using the information given here and the map on page 5, try to work out the possibilities and risks of escape from Siberia.

6 What do you know about Karl Marx whose books Trotsky was studying?

Part 2

The Empire at war

12 Petrograd in 1914

Meriel Buchanan was the daughter of the British Ambassador to Russia during World War One. Her diary, written in her early twenties, tells us much more about life in St Petersburg, the capital of Russia, in 1914. Its name was changed to Petrograd when war broke out, because the old name sounded too German.

The first extract describes 5 August 1914 when troops were leaving to fight Germany and Austria-Hungary at the start of World War One.

The second extract was written just four months later, in December, after the Russians had been defeated by Germany at the battles of Tannenberg and the Masurian Lakes. They were still fighting Austria in the Carpathian mountains which you can find on the map on page 29.

A 5 August 1914

The processions in the streets carrying the Emperor's portrait, framed in the flags of the Allies, the bands everywhere playing the National Anthem, the women and girls who flocked to the hospitals, the long unending lines of khaki-clad figures who marched away, singing and cheering; tall, bronzed men with honest, open faces, with childlike eyes, and a trusting faith in the Little Father, and a sure and certain hope that the saints would protect them and bring them safely back to their villages. Sometimes a woman would tramp along beside them, a shawl over her head and perhaps a child held in her tired patient arms, her eyes so worn out with weeping that now, when the actual moment of parting had come, she had no more tears to shed, could only stare hopelessly out into the emptiness of all the future days with the weary, dumb apathy of despair.

Those first days of the war! How full we were of enthusiasm, of the conviction that we were fighting in a just and holy cause, for the freedom and betterment of the world! Swept away by the general stir of excitement, we dreamt dreams of triumph and victory! The Russian Steam Roller! The British Navy! The French Guns! The war would be over by Christmas . . .

From M. Buchanan, *Dissolution of an Empire*, John Murray, 1932.

B December 1914

Grey days of biting cold, the silence of the snow hushing the bustling activity of the city to a sudden, almost disconcerting quiet. No balls, no music, no At Home days*, no ladies in Court dress wrapped in furs, no officers in gala uniform hurrying to a reception at the palace. The men we had danced with last year had lost their lives in East Prussia or were fighting in the Carpathians, the women were working in hospitals, in field ambulances, in Red Cross trains. War! We knew the meaning of it now in all its bitter, cruel truth! There were no cheering crowds about the streets, no flags carried round in procession, no bands playing the National Anthem outside the windows. Only silent throngs on the Nevski* reading the telegrams posted up on the shop-windows, girls in nurses' dress hurrying to duty, men with grave faces discussing the situation in low voices, women in mourning with dull, heavy eyes, bands of wounded soldiers being taken round and shown the town.

From M. Buchanan, *Dissolution of an Empire,* John Murray, 1932.

* when fashionable ladies were at home to see visitors

* the main street in Petrograd

Questions

1 What does the first extract tell you about the mood of the Russian people when they entered the war?

2 What evidence does the first passage give about the combination of forces which was expected to defeat Germany?

3 Do you think similar scenes would have been found in Berlin, Paris and London?

4 'Little Father' was a term used by poor Russians to describe the Tsar right through the Empire's history. What does it tell you about the way the country was governed?

5 Use the map on page 29 to find the battles in east Prussia and the Carpathians, both mentioned in the second passage.

6 How had the mood of the Russians changed by December 1914?

13 At the front?

In the first autumn of the war, Russian troops invaded Germany. Source B is a photograph of Russian soldiers in a German town in the early weeks of war. These men do not seem to have been involved in fighting but other parts of the army had already been defeated at the battles of Tannenburg and the Masurian Lakes.

Source A describes the condition of the wounded men and the general state of the army a few weeks after these defeats. It is written by M. V. Rodzianko who was President of the Duma, the Russian parliament which had been set up in 1905 but allowed very little power. Civil servants tried to stop men like Rodzianko from organising help for the wounded men and the army. But they could not prevent him going to visit troops in Poland, which was then in western Russia. There Rodzianko visited wounded men with Vyrubov, another politician.

The account of his visit to Poland is taken from Rodzianko's memoirs which he wrote after the war.

A Conditions in the army

Soon after the first battles, shocking reports came from the front of the incompetency of the sanitary department, of its inability to handle the wounded at the front. There was great confusion. Freight trains came to Moscow filled with wounded, lying on the bare floor, without even straw, in many cases without clothing, poorly bandaged, and unfed. . . .

The War Department was particularly weak in first aid. Though it had neither carts, horses, nor first aid material, yet it allowed no other organization on the field. . . .

Soon after my arrival at Warsaw in November, 1914, I had a call from Vyrubov, who asked me to go with him to the Warsaw–Vienna Station where there were about eighteen thousand men, wounded in the battles near Lodz and Berezina. There I saw a frightful scene. On the floor, without even a bedding of straw, in mud and slush, lay innumerable wounded, whose pitiful groans and cries filled the air. 'For God's sake, get them to attend to us. No one has looked after our wounds for five days.'

It should be said that after these bloody battles the wounded were thrown into freight cars without order, and thrown out at this station without attention. . . .

While at Warsaw, I asked permission of Grand Duke Nicholas Nicholaevich to go to Headquarters. I wished to tell him what I had seen and heard at Warsaw. General Ruzski had complained to me of lack of ammunition and the poor equipment of the men. There was a great shortage of boots. In the Carpathians, the soldiers fought barefooted. . . .

The Grand Duke stated that he was obliged to stop fighting, temporarily, for lack of ammunition and boots.

'You have influence,' he said. 'You are trusted. Try and get boots for the army, as soon as possible.'

From F. A. Golder, *Documents of Russian History 1914–1917*, The Century Co. (NY), 1927.

B Russian troops

Russian troops pass through a German town in the autumn of 1914.

Questions

1 What uses can you see being made of horses in the photograph?

2 What does the photograph tell you about the attitude of the local townspeople to the Russians?

3 What evidence is there to show the time of the year when the photograph was taken?

4 Does the photograph suggest that these men had or had not been fighting?

5 What examples are given by Rodzianko of the 'incompetency' of the sanitary (or health) department?

6 Find Lodz and Warsaw on the map on page 29. Do their positions help you to understand the difficulties of the war department?

7 Do you think the soldiers Rodzianko wrote about would have been an effective fighting force? Give reasons for your answer.

8 What problems faced by the army suggest that Russian industry was not able to cope with the needs of war-time?

9 Imagine you were Rodzianko and that you carried a notebook on your tour. Write down what you would have noted while visiting Lodz and interviewing the generals.

14 World War One

The map shows the front lines in December 1916. At the start of the war Russian armies had invaded Germany but were defeated at the battles of Tannenberg and the Masurian Lakes in August 1914. Later that year they had been driven out of western Poland and in 1915 were forced to retreat almost to the line shown on the map.

The war against Austria-Hungary centred on Galicia. The Russians won Galicia in the winter of 1914. They were forced out in 1915 but regained it in 1916.

Turkey entered the war, a month after it started, on the side of Germany and Austria-Hungary. In 1915 Britain tried to open another front on the shores of the Dardanelles, so that the Allies could defeat Turkey and open supply routes to Russia. The attempt failed.

Source B shows a very different view of Russia's armies from that given by Rodzianko in Source 13. The artist has painted a picture of healthy, well-equipped men who are devoted to their emperor and to their religion.

A   The Tsar with his troops

A painting of the Tsar Nicholas II blessing his troops in September 1917. He is holding an ikon, or holy picture.

B The front lines in 1916

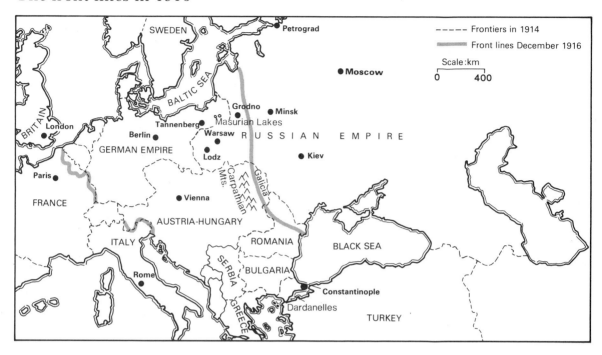

Questions

1 How far is it from Petrograd to the front line? What problems would this create for the Russian commanders?

2 What was the greatest number of kilometres by which Germany had invaded the Russian empire? How much of Austrian land had been gained by the Russians?

3 Using the map, explain how the British scheme to break through the Dardanelles could have helped Russia.

4 Imagine you are a British or French general. Why would you hope for strong Russian attacks on the Eastern Front?

5 What does the position of the front line in 1916 tell you about the successes and failures of the Russians in the war?

6 Are there any ways in which you can tell that the picture in Source A is a painting and not a photograph?

7 What does it suggest about the condition and equipment of the army?

8 Compare illustration A with Rodzianko's account of troops given in Source 13. In what ways do they tell different stories about the state of the army?

15 A Russian village in 1916

This is a report to the Tsar from a relative who owned most of the land in several villages. Here he reports on a village which was in western Russia where most of the grain needed to feed the cities was grown. It was far enough away from the front line to be able to give shelter to refugees from the provinces, or guberniias, in the war zone. The chief towns of the guberniias are marked on the map on page 29.

A Grushevka village

August 8, 1916
Grushevka

Complete statistics of losses in men in our Russian villages could not be obtained. For the present, I have data only for one village, that of Grushevka. The figures are: 115 (10 killed, 34 wounded, 71 missing or in captivity) out of 829 souls mobilized. Consequently, for the village of Grushevka the losses amount to 13 per cent of the total population of 3,307 souls, of whom 829 souls were in the army. In the village of Grushevka alone, more than five hundred petitions have been presented by widows, wives, and mothers of soldiers in active duty. They are getting allowances regularly, but the widows of the killed soldiers decorated with the order of St. George have thus far received nothing. I have collected all the information and turned it over to the proper authorities. We have also a goodly number of refugees: the largest percentage comes from Kholm guberniia, but there are also refugees from Grodno and Minsk guberniias. They all receive allowances regularly.

The grain harvest is good – in some places all that can be desired. Harvesting and threshing are going on everywhere, and there is hope that the work will be finished on time in the fall. In addition to women, children, and the aged, I have working for me 36 people from the Kherson jail, and 947 Austrian war prisoners. There are no Germans . . .

I shall probably remain at Grushevka until the 20th of August, i.e. three whole weeks. The air is incomparable. Space galore. Cannot see the horizon. Fields, fields . . . without end. At dawn I hunt anything that comes along. So far, with the aid of six urchins who beat the bushes, I have bagged six foxes, fourteen quail, and eight partridges.

From F. A. Golder, *Documents of Russian History 1914–1917*, The Century Co. (NY), 1927.

B Russian prisoners

Defeat. Russian prisoners with armed German or Austrian soldiers in May 1915.

Questions

1 Draw a block graph or pie diagram to show what happened to the men of Grushevka who joined the army. Show how many were killed, wounded, missing or taken prisoner.

2 Use the same kind of diagram to show how the population of Grushevka was made up in 1916. Show the original population (minus the soldiers), the men from jail and the prisoners of war.

3 Find the chief towns of the three guberniias on the map on page 29. Why were there so many refugees from them?

4 Why would the government need reports from villages?

5 Can you suggest reasons why there were no German prisoners in the village?

6 Imagine you were a peasant man or woman in Grushevka. What would you have thought of the nobleman? Use the information in the document for your answer.

7 What does the photograph tell you about some of the Russian soldiers who may have been taken into the army from villages like Grushevka?

8 If you were one of the prisoners in the picture, what do you think your feelings would be after you had surrendered?

16 The Tsar at Headquarters

Tsar Nicholas II spent much of his time at Headquarters and, in August 1915, made himself Commander-in-Chief of the Russian armies. These letters to his wife show the many difficulties of the Russian troops and their officers.

A Letters from the Tsar

2 December 1914

. . . The only great and serious difficulty for our army is again the lack of ammunition. Because of that our troops are obliged, while fighting, to be cautious and to economize. This means that the burden of fighting falls on the infantry. As a result our losses are enormous. Some army corps have shrunk to divisions, brigades to companies, etc.

From F. A. Golder, *Documents of Russian History 1914–1917*, The Century Co. (NY), 1927.

2 July 1915

. . . Owing to the heat we take long rides in automobiles and go very little on foot. We selected new districts and explored the surrounding country, being guided by our maps. Often we made mistakes because the maps we have were made eighteen years ago and since then some of the forests have disappeared while new woods and new villages have appeared . . .

7 July 1915

. . . Again that cursed question of shortage of artillery and rifle ammunition – it stands in the way of an energetic advance. If we should have three days of serious fighting we might run out of ammunition altogether. Without new rifles, it is impossible to fill up the gaps. The army is now almost stronger than in peace time; it should be (and was at the beginning) three times as strong. This is the situation in which we find ourselves at present.

If we had a rest from fighting for about a month, our condition would greatly improve. It is understood, of course, that what I say is strictly for you only. Please do not say a word of this to any one.

15 March 1916

Such a great thaw has set in that the positions occupied by our troops where we have moved forward are flooded with water knee-deep, so that it is impossible either to sit or lie down in the trenches. The roads are rapidly deteriorating; the artillery and the transport are scarcely moving. Even the bravest troops cannot fight under such conditions, when it is impossible even to dig trenches. As a result our attack had to be stopped.

24 July 1916

The most important and immediate question is fuel and metal – iron and copper for ammunition. Without metals the mills cannot supply a sufficient amount of bullets and bombs. The same is true in regard to the railways. Trepov [Minister of Transportation] assures me that the railways work better this year than last and produces proof, but nevertheless every one complains that they are not doing as well as they might.

Questions

1 Make a list of the weaknesses in Russia's fighting strength described by the Tsar. At the side of each point make a note of other evidence for the same weakness, taking your evidence from Sources 12 to 15.

2 Can you explain why lack of ammunition led to serious losses among the ordinary foot soldiers or infantry?

3 In what ways would it be true to say that the problems of the army really started in the factories?

4 Which season of the year was the worst for fighting? Give a reason for your answer.

5 Imagine you were a Russian soldier fighting in World War One. Write a letter home to your family telling them what life at the front was like.

Part 3

The Republic
March–November 1917

17 The week before revolution

The map shows how Petrograd was divided by the River Neva. To the north lay the factories and huddled homes of the working class. To the south were the fine public buildings, churches and the barracks for several regiments.

On 12 March 1917 there was a revolution in Petrograd. The extract describes what was happening in the week before as it was remembered by Leon Trotsky who played a leading part in the Communist revolution six months later. In March 1917 he was in a Canadian prison but he returned to Petrograd shortly afterwards.

A Petrograd in 1917

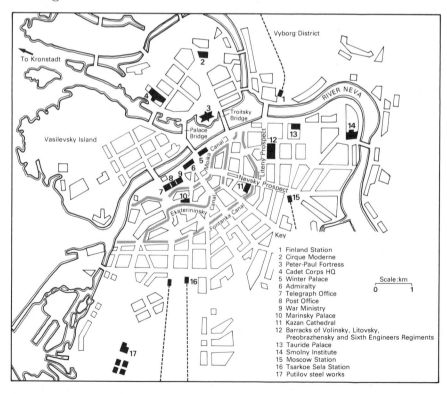

Key

1 Finland Station
2 Cirque Moderne
3 Peter-Paul Fortress
4 Cadet Corps HQ
5 Winter Palace
6 Admiralty
7 Telegraph Office
8 Post Office
9 War Ministry
10 Marinsky Palace
11 Kazan Cathedral
12 Barracks of Volinsky, Litovsky,
   Preobrazhensky and Sixth Engineers Regiments
13 Tauride Palace
14 Smolny Institute
15 Moscow Station
16 Tsarkoe Sela Station
17 Putilov steel works

Scale:km
0   1

B Leon Trotsky

8 March (Thursday)
About 90,000 workers, men and women, were on strike. The fighting mood expressed itself in demonstrations, meetings, encounters with the police. The movement began in the Vyborg district, with its large industrial establishments, then it crossed over to the Petersburg side.

From L. Trotsky, *History of the Russian Revolution*, vol. I, Gollancz, 1932.

9 March (Friday)
About one half of the industrial workers of Petrograd are on strike. . . . (197,000) The workers come to the factories in the morning; instead of going to work, they hold meetings; then begin the processions toward the centre . . .

Throughout the entire day, crowds of people poured from one part of the city to another. They were persistently dispelled by the police, stopped and crowded back by cavalry detachments and occasionally by the infantry.

10 March (Saturday)
. . . the strike spread wider . . . 240,000 workers participated that day. . . . Already a good number of small establishments are on strike. The street cars are at a standstill. Business concerns are closed. In the course of the day students of the higher schools join the strike. By noon, tens of thousands of people pour to the Kazan cathedral and the surrounding streets. Attempts are made to organize street meetings: a series of armed encounters with the police occur.

Questions

1 How is Petrograd linked with the interior of Russia by river and rail?

2 Do you notice anything about the position of the railway stations? Who used Tsarkoe Sela station? What was the importance of the Finland station for European travellers?

3 Which buildings would you most want to seize if you were planning a revolution? Give reasons for your answer.

4 Which group of people did Trotsky think was the most important in the disturbances?

5 By which routes would most of the demonstrators reach the city centre?

6 Does the evidence suggest that the strikers were protesting mostly against their employers or against the government?

18 The eve of revolution

This selection of extracts deals with the events of Sunday 11 March, the day before the Tsar's government was overthrown.

Meriel Buchanan's diary shows that by this time the trouble in the streets was getting out of hand, especially after a mutiny in the Pavlovsky Regiment. But the second extract shows that the Tsar and his wife had no idea of how serious the situation was. The President of the Duma knew better (Source C). He hoped to force the Tsar to set up a new government of elected members of the Duma to replace ministers chosen personally by the Tsar. Instead, the Tsar ordered the commander of the troops in Petrograd to put an end to the disorders. According to the eyewitness account in Source F the commander's efforts failed.

A Diary of Meriel Buchanan

It was a brilliantly fine day, and, in spite of the orders posted up at street corners forbidding the assembly of crowds, there had been massed processions of workmen and the Nevsky had been thronged with people. . . . Some of the troops had fired on the crowds, but the Pavlovsky had refused to obey the order of their officers and had had to be disbanded.

From M. Buchanan, *Dissolution of an Empire*, John Murray, 1932

B Letter from the Tsarina to the Tsar

The whole trouble comes from these idlers, well-dressed people, wounded soldiers, high-school girls etc. . . . Lily spoke to some cab-drivers to find out about things. They told her that the students came to them and told them that if they appeared in the streets in the morning, they would be shot to death. What corrupt minds! Of course the cab-drivers and the motormen are now on strike. But they say it is all different from 1905 because they all worship you and only want bread.

From *Krasny Archiv*, vol. IV, published in USSR, 1923.

C Telegram from the President of the Duma to the Tsar

The situation is serious. The Capital is in a state of anarchy. The Government is paralyzed; the transport service is broken down; the food and fuel supplies are completely disorganized. Discontent is general and on the increase. There is wild shooting on the streets; troops are firing at each other. It is urgent that someone enjoying the confidence of the country be entrusted with the formation of a new Government.

From F. A. Golder, *Documents of Russian History 1914–1917*, The Century Co. (NY), 1927.

D Telegram from the Tsar to the Commander of forces in Petrograd

I command you to put an end as from tomorrow to all disturbances in the streets.

E Notice by the Commander of troops in Petrograd

NOTICE

In the past few days there had been disturbances in Petrograd in which attempts have been made on the lives of soldiers and police. I forbid any meetings in the streets. I warn the people of Petrograd that the military have instructions from me to use their rifles and be ruthless in taking measures to return order in the capital.

The Commander of the Petrograd Defence Committee
Lieutenant-general KHABALOV

From W. Astrov (ed.), *Illustrated History of the Russian Revolution*, M. Lawrence, 1928.

F An eyewitness account of soldiers' behaviour

On the bridge, shoulder to shoulder and barring the way, stood a cordon of Grenadiers. In spite of the presence of an officer, they were standing easy and conversing with the crowd on political topics . . . a few individuals filtered through without turning back. There was clearly nothing for the officers to do but turn a blind eye.

For this detachment to take aim and open fire on the people it had been conversing with was unthinkable, and no-one in the crowd believed for a moment it was possible. On the contrary, the soldiers obviously would not have objected if their front was broken through, and many of them would probably have shared their arms with the crowd.

From N. N. Sukhanov, (edited and translated by Joel Carmichael) *The Russian Revolution*, OUP, 1955.

Questions

1 What two pieces of evidence does Meriel Buchanan give to show that the situation was becoming worse for the government?

2 Lily was a noble lady and friend of the Tsarina. How reliable do you think her opinions would be?

3 Imagine yourself to be the Tsar, 320 km from Petrograd, reading reports from your wife and from the President of the Duma. What differences would you see in the accounts? Which would you most want to believe?

4 Read the Tsar's telegram to the Commander. Do you think he thought the trouble was very serious?

5 Explain in your own words what the President of the Duma was suggesting in the last sentence of this telegram (Source C).

6 For what reasons does the eyewitness say the Grenadiers would have been unwilling to fire on the crowd? What does this account tell you about the effects of the Commander's public notice?

19 The day of revolution

During the night of 11–12 March 1917 many regiments decided to mutiny. Just after midnight, the President of the Duma again telegraphed the Tsar asking for 'measures to be taken immediately'. He meant that a new government should be chosen from members of the Duma. The Tsar did nothing.

The story is taken up by a socialist lawyer, Alexander Kerensky. He tells how members of the Duma went ahead and formed a new government. Here it is called the Provisional Committee; later it was known as the Provisional Government. The Duma's meeting place was the Tauride Palace (see map on page 34).

The same afternoon, a Soviet of Workers' Deputies was set up. 'Soviet' is the Russian word for council and the deputies were chosen by workers in different factories and districts. Sections of the army also sent deputies to the Soviet.

A Telegram from the President of the Duma to the Tsar

The situation is growing worse. Measures should be taken immediately, as tomorrow will be too late. The last hour has struck, when the fate of the country and dynasty is being decided.

B Alexander Kerensky

8.00 a.m. . . . at about eight o'clock in the morning, I was awakened by a voice saying: 'Get up! Nekrasov is on the telephone. . . . the Volinsk Regiment has mutinied and is leaving its barracks. You are wanted at the Duma at once. . . .'

I jumped up, dressed quickly and hurried to the Duma . . . a five minute walk. . . .

8.30 a.m. At about half past eight I arrived at the small side entrance (the library entrance) of the Tauride Palace, seat of the Duma.

From A. Kerensky, *The Catastrophe*, Appleton & Co. (NY), 1927.

C Formation of a Provisional Committee

As soon as I appeared in the hall, I was surrounded by people and bombarded with questions. I told them that there were riots all over the city, that the insurgent* troops were on their way to the Duma and that I knew the Revolution had begun. I said that . . . it was our duty to welcome them and to make common cause with them . . . at the unofficial session which met from 12.00 to 2.00 but the decision was made to form a Provisional Committee with unrestricted powers. . . .

3.00 p.m. By three o'clock that afternoon the Duma was unrecognisable. It was packed with civilians and soldiers. . . . The reports came in at a bewildering rate. Hundreds of people wanted attention, gave advice and asked for work. . . . We had to keep our heads, for it would have been disastrous to waste precious time or show any lack of self-confidence. We had to decide on the spot what answers to give, what orders to issue, when to encourage . . . where to send troops and reinforcements, how to find room for the hundreds of people being arrested . . .

From A. Kerensky, *The Kerensky Memoirs*, Cassell & Co., 1966.

* rebellious

4.00 p.m. . . . someone came to see about finding space in the Tauride Palace for the Soviet of Workers' Deputies, which had also just been formed . . . Room 13 was turned over to them, and they convened their first meeting there without delay. . . .

By sundown . . . the entire city of Petrograd was in the hands of insurgent troops. The former government machinery had ceased to operate, and some of the ministry buildings and government offices had been occupied by revolutionaries. Other buildings, such as the headquarters of the secret police, the police stations, and the law courts, had been set on fire. Inside the Duma we had by now set up a central body to control the troops and the insurgents.

D The revolution on the streets

This photograph was taken on 12 March 1917 and shows barricades in a Petrograd street.

Questions

1 What did the Duma President mean by his telegram?

2 According to Alexander Kerensky, what part did he play in turning the riots and mutinies into a revolution?

3 What phrase in Kerensky's description makes it clear that the Provisional Committee took over the Tsar's government?

4 Can you think of any reason why the workers were so quick to call the first Soviet?

5 In Source C who does Kerensky say was in charge of Petrograd?

6 In what ways does the photograph illustrate some of the facts given in these extracts?

7 What was the purpose of the boxes between the cannon?

20 The Provisional Government's first meeting

The Provisional Government was formed by leading members of the old Duma. A few of its members, such as its chairman, Prince Lvov, were noblemen but most were businessmen and lawyers from Petrograd and Moscow. The only socialist among them was the lawyer, Alexander Kerensky. Here he describes the many problems the government had to face immediately after it had taken power from the emperor's government – 'the autocracy'.

Source D is a photograph of the main meeting room in the Duma building, the Tauride Palace, taken before the revolution. The Tauride Palace had many other rooms where ministers had their offices and one where the Soviet meetings took place.

A The Provisional Government

It inherited nothing from the autocracy but a terrible war, an acute food shortage, a paralysed transportation system, an empty treasury, and a population in a state of furious discontent and anarchic disintegration. . . .

From A. Kerensky, *The Catastrophe*, Appleton & Co. (NY), 1927.

B The first meeting

Prince Lvov read to us at our first meeting a report on the situation in the provinces. From all towns and cities, provincial and county seats came telegrams. . . . They all told the same story: the old administration from the governor to the last town policeman and village bailiff had disappeared without trace, and everywhere were being formed, instead, all sorts of self-appointed organizations – Soviets, committees of public safety etc. . . .

The villages, liberated from all administrative vigilance, had begun to 'govern themselves'. There was an immediate mad rush by the peasantry for the land.

In the cities, various self-appointed organizations, whipped up by the raging revolutionary tempest, were devoting themselves to such creative revolutionary activities as raids, searches, confiscations and the liberation not only of political prisoners but also of criminals. . . .

From A. Kerensky, *The Kerensky Memoirs*, Cassell & Co., 1966.

C Other business

Apart from passing legislation, the government also had to conduct the war and cope with innumerable day-to-day administrative questions. Moreover, there was an endless procession of visitors and delegations, representatives of the new local administrative bodies, and of the national minorities, constantly crowding the halls of the Marinsky

From A. Kerensky, *The Kerensky Memoirs*, Cassell & Co., 1966.

Palace* and the offices of the individual ministers. It was an unbeliev-
ably hectic time of endless cabinet meetings by day and by night, and
of all kinds of conferences and addresses to mass meetings.

** one of the
government offices*

D The Duma

A view of the Duma at work, taken from the back of the hall, facing the Presidential chair.

Questions

1 Describe in your own words the situation in Russia when the Provisional Government took over.

2 What would most have worried you about this situation if you were a member of the Provisional Government?

3 What kind of 'administrative vigilance' had disappeared from the villages?

4 What is meant by 'there was an immediate rush by the peasants for the land'?

5 What do you think is Kerensky's attitude to the events he describes in the fourth paragraph, beginning 'In the cities'?

6 Look at the photograph of the Duma in Source D.
   a) Why do you think the seating was arranged in this way?
   b) How were the powers of the Duma different from those of the Provisional Government?

21 The Soviet

The Soviet of Workers' and Soldiers' Deputies was set up in the Duma building on the same day as the Provisional Government. It aimed to protect the interests of the workers and prevent the Provisional Government falling under the influence of noblemen, army officers and other people who had been loyal to the Tsar. At first Alexander Kerensky was the only member of the Soviet who was also in the Provisional Government.

Sources A and B are proclamations made by the Soviet on the first day it met. They show that the Soviet was determined to be organised and armed well enough to stand up to the new government. Military Order No. 1 (Source C) came two days later. In it the Soviet leaders call on the troops to be loyal to them first and their officers or the government second.

A The Soviet is called (12 March)

CITIZENS: The representatives of the workers, soldiers, and inhabitants of Petrograd, meeting in the State Duma, announce that the first session of their representatives will take place at seven o'clock tonight in the building of the State Duma. All those troops that have joined the side of the people should immediately elect their representatives, one for each company. Factory workers should elect one deputy for each one thousand. Factories with less than one thousand workers should elect one deputy each.

From A. F. Golder, *Documents of Russian History 1914–1917*, The Century Co. (NY), 1927.

B A message to the workers (12 March)

The working class is greatly in need of guns. The success of the fight is closely bound up with the organization and arming of the workers. Therefore, the Soviet of Workers' Deputies asks all comrade-workers who have guns, to hand them over to the commissars appointed by the Soviet for the different wards of the capital. If for some reason this is not possible, then deliver them to the Soviet which meets in the building of the State Duma.

From A. F. Golder, *Documents of Russian History 1914–1917*, The Century Co. (NY), 1927.

C Soviet Military Order No. 1 (14 March)

The Soviet of Workers' and Soldiers' Deputies has resolved:
1. In all companies, battalions, regiments, . . . batteries, squadrons, . . . and on the vessels of the navy, committees from the elected representatives of the lower ranks . . . shall be chosen immediately.
2. In all those military units which have not yet chosen their representatives to the Soviet of Workers' Deputies, one representative from each company shall be selected. . .
3. In all its political actions, the military branch is subordinated to the Soviet of Workers' and Soldiers' Deputies. . .

From A. F. Golder, *Documents of Russian History 1914–1917*, The Century Co. (NY), 1927.

4. The orders of . . . the State Duma shall be executed only in such cases as do not conflict with the orders . . . of the Soviet of Workers' and Soldiers' Deputies.

5. All kinds of arms, such as rifles, machine-guns, armoured automobiles, and others, must be kept . . . under the control of the company and battalion committees, and in no case be turned over to officers, even at their demand.

6. . . .soldiers cannot in any way be deprived of those rights which all citizens enjoy. In particular, standing at attention and compulsory saluting, when not on duty, is abolished.

7. Also, the addressing of the officers with the title, 'Your Excellency', 'Your Honour', etc., is abolished and these titles are replaced by the address of 'Mister General', 'Mister Colonel', etc.

Questions

1 From your reading of these extracts what do you understand by the following words: (a) Soviet; (b) deputy; (c) commissar?

2 What is the difference between the way the Soviet was elected and the way in which the British parliament or local council is elected?

3 Why did the Soviet leaders state that the working class needed guns in Source B?

4 What does Source B tell you about the Soviet attitude to the Provisional Government?

5 Imagine a conversation between two officers reading Military Order No. 1. How do you think they would have reacted to the order?

6 Section 4 in Source C speaks of the State Duma but it really refers to the Provisional Government who had taken control of the country on the Duma's behalf. What does this section tell you about the likely future loyalty of the army to the country's new rulers?

22 The peasants' revolt

After the March Revolution many peasants believed that the new government would allow them to take land from their landlords and divide it between them. But the Provisional Government was too afraid of making enemies of the landowners to put forward a scheme for land reform. In the autumn of 1917, villagers began to take the law into their own hands and started to seize land. This often led to riots and fights. This report is taken from the Soviet's newspaper, Izvestia *('News'), of 1 August 1917.*

A Village of Teliazh, Orlov* Guberniia

Each year the peasants rented their land from the landholder. This year they went to him as usual and he asked the usual rent. The peasants refused to pay it, and without much bargaining went home. There they called a meeting and decided to take up the land without paying. They put the ploughs and harrows on their carts and started for the field. When they arrived, they got into an argument as to the division of the land because it was not all the same quality. When they had quarrelled for a time, one of the party proposed that they proceed to the landholder's warehouse, where some good alcohol was kept. They broke into the place, where they found fifty barrels. They drank and drank, but could not drink it all. They became so drunk that they did not know what they were doing and carelessly set the place on fire. Four burned to death; the ninety others escaped. A few days later they returned to the field and once more quarrelled. It ended in a fight in which thirteen were left dead, fifteen were carried off badly injured, and, of these, four died.

Soon after that a quarrel started over the rich peasants. In the village there were eighteen farmers who had from twenty-five to thirty dessiatins* of land. They had a reserve of grain of various kinds. About thirty of the villagers seized this reserve. Another village meeting was called. A few of the more intelligent peasants came out strongly against this act of robbery. It ended in another fight in which three were killed and five badly wounded. One of these peasants, whose son was killed, shook his fist and shouted, 'I will make you pay for my son'.

From A. F. Golder, *Documents of Russian History 1914–1917*, The Century Co. (NY), 1927.

* now called Berezniki. It is on the River Kama, just west of the Urals

* approximately one hectare

B A meeting of peasants, April 1917

Peasants meet in the village of Dobrovody, expecting to share out the landowners' lands among themselves

Questions

1 If events like this were taking place all over Russia, what effect would they have on the position of the Provisional Government?

2 If you were a revolutionary wishing to overthrow the Provisional Government, what promise would you make to the peasants?

3 What does the extract tell you about divisions amongst the peasantry? Do you think these divisions were likely to become important?

4 Using the information in this passage, try to estimate the total population of Teliazh. Explain how you reached your answer.

5 What do the photograph and the extract suggest about the peasantry's feelings towards the Provisional Government in the spring and autumn of 1917?

23 A protest meeting

By October, complaints against the Provisional Government could be heard every-where in Petrograd. Soldiers argued that the Provisional Government should have made peace with Germany and that the war went on only to make profits for the wealthy businessmen (or 'capitalists') and to win Russia new lands, including the Turkish port of Constantinople. There were criticisms that the army had not changed since Tsarist days. An American journalist, John Reed, wrote this account of a meeting at the Cirque Moderne, a circus building in the working class district of north Petrograd.

A Soldiers' speeches

I went across the river to the Cirque Moderne, to one of the great popular meetings which took place all over the city, more numerous night after night. The bare, gloomy, amphi-theatre, lit by five tiny lights hanging from a thin wire, was packed from the ring up the steep sweep of grimy benches to the very roof – soldiers, sailors, workmen, women, all listening as if their lives depended on it. A soldier was speaking . . .

From J. Reed, *Ten Days That Shook the World*, Martin Lawrence, 1932.

'Comrades , he cried, and there was real anguish in his drawn face and despairing gestures. 'The people at the top are always calling upon us to sacrifice more, sacrifice more than those who have everything and are left unmolested.

'We are at war with Germany. Would we invite German generals to serve on our staff? Well, we're at war with the capitalists too, and yet invite them into our Government.'

The soldier says, 'Show me what I'm fighting for. Is it Constanti-nople, or is it free Russia? Is it the democracy, or is it the capitalist plunderers? If you can prove to me that I am defending the Revolution, then I'll go out and fight without capital punishment to force me.

'When the land belongs to the peasants, and the factories to the workers and the power to the Soviets, then we'll know we have some-thing to fight for, and we'll fight for it!' . . .

The spokesman for the Eighth Army:

'We are weak, we have only a few men left in each company. They must give us food and boots and reinforcements, or soon there will be left only empty trenches. Peace or supplies . . . either let the Govern-ment end the war or support the Army.'

For the Forty-sixth Siberian Artillery:

'The officers will not work with our Committees . . . they apply the death penalty to our agitators and the counter-Revolutionary Govern-ment supports them. We thought that the Revolution would bring peace. But now the Government forbids us even to talk of such things, and at the same time doesn't give us enough food to live on, or enough ammunition to fight with.'

B Distributing pamphlets in Moscow, August 1917

Crowds picking up pamphlets, scattered by the Bolshevik Party, protesting at the policies of Kerensky's government. Notice that many well-to-do people are reading the pamphlets.

Questions

1 What ideas used in the first soldier's speech tell us that he is a socialist?

2 Who were 'the people at the top' referred to by the first soldier?

3 The first soldier says that he is ready to fight to defend the Revolution. What does he mean by 'revolution'?

4 What does the spokesman for the Eighth Army suggest will happen if the government does not make peace or give the army supplies?

5 From your reading of these accounts, how much support do you think the Provisional Government would get if it was faced with a revolution?

6 What does the Artilleryman mean by 'counter-revolutionary'?

7 What does his speech tell you about the working of Soviet Military Order No 1 (printed in Source 21)?

8 Do John Reed's reports and the photograph tell you anything about how far the Bolshevik Party was able to campaign in the open rather than as a secret underground group?

Part 4

The Bolsheviks

24 A revolutionary's life

Vladimir Ilyich Ulyanov was born in 1870. In 1887 his brother, Alexander, was hanged for attempting to kill the Tsar. The next year Vladimir went to University but within a few weeks had been expelled after taking part in a demonstration. He studied at home and finally passed his law examinations. When he went to St Petersburg in 1893 he became active in illegal socialist organisations. The story is taken up by a woman socialist, Nadezhda Krupskaya, who later became Vladimir's wife. She tells first how she and Vladimir had been involved in revolutionary underground activities (A), followed by two years in prison (B) and then exile in Siberia (C). Here they lived near the River Lena and this gave Vladimir the revolutionary name of Lenin which he used for the rest of his life.

A Revolutionary work

We divided the work up, according to districts. . . . A leaflet was got out for the women workers of the Laferme Tobacco factory. . . . They rolled up the leaflets into little tubes so that they could easily be taken one by one and arranged them in their aprons in a suitable manner. Then, immediately the hooter sounded, they walked briskly towards the women who were pouring out in throngs from the factory gates and, passing by almost at a trot, scattered the leaflets right into the hands of the perplexed workers.

From N. Krupskaya, *Memories of Lenin,* Martin Lawrence, 1930.

B Life in prison

Vladimir Ilyich was arrested in December 1895. He spent two years in prison, but carried on studying and writing as well as keeping in touch with his comrades. . . . Letters written in milk came through from outside on the day for sending books – Saturday. One would immediately look at the secret signs in the book and ascertain whether a letter was inside. At six o'clock they brought hot water for tea and the wardress led the criminals out to the Church. By this time the 'politicals' would have the letters torn into long strips. The they would make their tea, and as soon as the wardress departed begin to drop the strips into the hot tea. Thus the letters would be 'developed'. . . . Just as Vladimir Ilyich was the pivot of all our work outside, so in prison he

From N. Krupskaya, *Memories of Lenin,* Martin Lawrence, 1930.

was the centre of contact with the outside world. But apart from this he did a great deal of work in prison. . . . 'It is a pity they let us out so soon,' he said jokingly. 'I would have liked to do a little more work on the book. It will be difficult to obtain books in Siberia'. . . . In order not to be discovered while writing with milk, he made little milk-'inkpots' out of bread. These he popped into his mouth immediately he heard a rattle at the grating. 'To-day I have eaten six ink-pots,' ran the post-script to one of his letters.

C Exile in Siberia

We hired half a house with yard and kitchen-garden attached, for four roubles. We lived as one family. In the summer it was impossible to find anyone to help with the housework. I and another together fought with the Russian stove. At first I knocked over with the oven-hook the soup and dumplings, which were scattered over the hearth. But after-wards I got used to it. . . . Exile did not pass so badly. Those were years of serious study. The nearer we approached the end of the period of exile, Vladimir Ilyich gave more and more thought to future work. . . . For all practical purposes there was no Party, and no printing press. . . . It was necessary to begin with the organisation of an all-Russian newspaper, to establish it abroad, to connect it up as closely as possible with activities in Russia, to arrange transport in the best way possible. Vladimir Ilyich began to spend sleepless nights. He became terribly thin.

From N. Krupskaya, *Memories of Lenin*, Martin Lawrence, 1930.

Questions

1 What sort of messages might be written in the leaflets distributed to the factory workers?

2 What do you think was the difference between a political and criminal prisoner?

3 Describe how Lenin spent his time in prison. How did he keep in touch with the comrades outside?

4 In what ways was exile in Siberia different from being in prison?

5 Why was a printing press so important to the work of a revolutionary?

6 Why would it be necessary to establish the newspaper abroad?

7 From your reading of these extracts what do you think were Lenin's strengths as a revolutionary leader?

25 Lenin's return to Russia, 1917

While Lenin was in exile in Siberia, a Russian socialist party was formed illegally. But Lenin quarrelled with its aims, saying it concentrated on trying to win better conditions for workers instead of overthrowing the government of the Empire. The party split in 1903 and Lenin was left as leader of a small group of revolutionary socialists known as Bolsheviks.

From 1907 to 1917 Lenin was an émigré – a wanted man who did not dare to live in Russia. In 1917 he was in Zurich, Switzerland, while his country was at war with Germany. News came of the 'February Revolution' which overthrew the Tsar. (According to the Western Calendar this happened on 12 March.) The story is told by his wife, Nadezhda Krupskaya.

A   News of the revolution reaches Lenin

From the moment news of the February revolution came, Ilyich burned with eagerness to go to Russia. England and France would not for the world have allowed the Bolsheviks to pass through to Russia. . . . As there was no legal way it was necessary to travel illegally. But how? From the moment the news of the revolution came, Ilyich did not sleep and at night all sorts of incredible plans were made. . . .

. . . On March 19th there was a meeting of the Russian political emigré groups in Switzerland . . . to discuss ways and means of getting back to Russia. Martov* presented a plan to obtain permits for emigrants to pass through Germany in exchange for German and Austrian prisoners of war interned in Russia. But no one wanted to go that way, except Lenin, who snatched at this plan.

When news came that the German Government would give Lenin and his friends safe passage through Germany in a 'sealed train' Lenin wanted to leave at once.

'We will take the first train.' The train was due to leave within two hours. We had just these two hours to liquidate our entire 'household', settle accounts with the landlady, return the books to the library, pack up and so on. 'Go yourself, I will leave tomorrow,' I said. But Ilyich insisted, 'No, we will go together.' In the two hours everything was done: books packed, letters destroyed, the necessary clothing and things chosen, and all affairs settled. . .

In boarding the train, no questions were asked about the baggage and passports, Ilyich kept entirely to himself, his thoughts were in Russia. En route, the conversation was mainly trivial. . . . On arrival in Berlin our train was shunted on to a siding. . . . On March 31st we

From N. Krupskaya,
Memories of Lenin,
Martin Lawrence, 1930.

* *an old political friend of Lenin. They later quarrelled*

arrived in Sweden. . . . A red flag was hung up in the waiting-room and a meeting was held. . . . From Sweden we crossed to Finland in small Finnish sledges. Everything was already familiar and dear to us – the wretched third-class cars, the Russian soldiers. It was terribly good. . . . Our people were huddled against the windows. The station platforms we passed were crowded with soldiers. Usyevich leaned out of the window and shouted: 'Long live the world revolution!' The soldiers looked at him puzzled.

Ilyich asked the comrades who sat with us if we would be arrested on our arrival; they smiled. Soon we arrived in Petrograd.

The Petrograd masses, workers, soldiers and sailors came to meet their leader. . . . There was a sea of people all around.

Questions

1 Why were Lenin and the other Bolsheviks so eager to return to Russia?

2 Why did many of the émigrés not like Martov's plan to travel through Germany?

3 What reason is given in the passage for the Germans helping Lenin to return home? What other reasons might they have had?

4 Why should the soldiers in Finland be puzzled at the slogan shouted through the window?

5 The 'Petrograd masses' welcomed Lenin, according to his wife. How reliable do you think her statement is? Give reasons for your answer.

6 What do you think would have been the views about Lenin's return held by (a) the Provisional Government and (b) the Soviet?

26 The eve of revolution

Six months after his return to Russia in April 1917, Lenin persuaded the Bolshevik Party to lead a revolution, acting in the name of the workers' Soviets, against the Provisional Government. The man responsible for planning the revolt was Trotsky, who had recently joined the Bolsheviks and had also been elected chairman of the Petrograd Soviet. He had the help of the Military Revolutionary Committee (or 'the Committee') whose headquarters were the Bolshevik meeting place in the Smolny Institute. The headquarters of the Provisional Government was now the Winter Palace.

A Trotsky's headquarters in the Smolny Institute

The twelfth hour of the revolution was near. The Smolny was being transformed into a fortress. In its garret there were a dozen or two machine guns. . .

From L. Trotsky, *My Life*, Butterworth, 1930.

November 6, a grey morning, early. I roamed about the building from one floor to another. . . to make sure that everything was in order and to encourage those who needed it. Along the stone floors of the interminable and still half-dark corridors of the Smolny, the soldiers were dragging their machine guns. . .

On the third floor of the Smolny, in a small corner room, the Committee was in continuous session. All the reports about the movement of troops, the attitude of soldiers and workers, the agitation in the barracks. . . .The happenings in the Winter Palace – all these came to this centre.

All that week I had hardly stepped out of the Smolny; I spent the nights on a leather couch without undressing, sleeping in snatches, and constantly being roused by couriers, scouts, messenger-cyclists, telegraphists, and ceaseless telephone calls.

On the night of the 6th, the members of the Revolutionary Committee went out into various districts, and I was left alone. Later on, Kamanev* came in. He was opposed to the uprising, but he had come to spend that deciding night with me, and together we stayed in the tiny corner room on the third floor, so like the captain's bridge on that deciding night of the revolution.

* a leading Bolshevik

B The workers prepare in the Vyborg district

The Vyborg district was preparing for the insurrection. There were fifty women workers in the premises of the Vyborg Council during the entire night, a woman doctor was giving them instructions in first aid. In the rooms of the district committee the workers were being armed: group after group came to the Committee and received rifles and ammunition.

From N. Krupskaya, *Memories of Lenin*, Martin Lawrence, 1930.

C The Navy prepares to help the Bolsheviks

Approximately 1,500 volunteers from various ships formed a landing party expedition, which went by train to Petrograd in order to support the Soviet.

The torpedo-boats have also provided fighting detachments.

From G. E. Vullicamy, *Red Archives*, G. Bles, 1929.

D The Soldiers take over the Barracks

An order was sent out through the garrison from Smolny...Officers not recognising the authority of the Military Revolutionary Committee to be arrested. The commanders of many regiments fled of their own accord. In other units the officers were removed and arrested.

From L. Trotsky, *History of the Russian Revolution*, Vol. III, Gollancz, 1932.

Questions

1 Find the Smolny on the map on page 34. What had it been before it became Bolshevik headquarters?

2 Where was the Vyborg district? Why was it an important centre of revolution?

3 Using the information in Source A to help you, describe how Trotsky organised the revolution. You might find it useful to draw a diagram showing some of the organisations he could call on.

4 Use the extracts to draw up a list of the different groups of people who were preparing to take part in the revolution.

5 Why was the support of sailors and soldiers so important to the revolutionaries?

6 Suggest reasons why so many troops turned against the government.

7 How did rebellious troops deal with officers loyal to the Provisional Government?

27 The night of revolution

By the early morning of 7 November the Bolsheviks had enough armed men under their command to take over the city. Some were Red Guards or bands of armed workers; others were army soldiers who came over to the side of the revolutionaries. In the first source John Reed describes the scene in the Smolny as the action began. In Sources B and C Trotsky tells of the take-over of key points. By this time Alexander Kerensky was prime minister and he describes, in Source D and E, how he failed to win support from troops.

A John Reed visits the Smolny

Towards four in the morning [of November 7] I met Zorin in the outer hall, a rifle slung from his shoulder.

'We're moving!' said he, calmly but with satisfaction. 'We pinched the Assistant Minister of Justice and the Minister of Religions. They're down in the cellar now. One regiment is on the march to capture the Telephone Exchange, another the Telegraph Agency, another the State Bank. The Red Guard is out. . . .'

On the steps of Smolny, in the chill dark, we first saw the Red Guard – a huddled group of boys in workmen's clothes, carrying guns with bayonets, talking nervously together.

From J. Reed, *Ten Days That Shook the World*, Martin Lawrence, 1926

B Military take-over

Peter and Paul Fortress . . . is today completely taken possession of. . . . Machine guns are set up on the fortress wall to command the quay and the Troitsky bridge. . . .

From L. Trotsky, *History of the Russian Revolution*, Vol. III, Gollancz, 1932.

C Taking over key points

The Military Revolutionary Committee sent a detachment of sailors to the Telephone Exchange, and the detachment placed two small guns at the entrance. . . . The telephone girls . . . fled with hysterical screams through the gates. . . . The sailors managed somehow to handle the work of the switchboard. Thus began the taking over of the organs of administration. . . .

At the railway terminals, specially appointed Commissaries are watching the incoming and outgoing trains. . .

From L. Trotsky, *My Life*, Butterworth, 1930

D Kerensky tries to defend the Government

We were waiting for troops to arrive from the Front. They had been summoned by me in good time and were due in Petrograd on the morning of November 7. But instead of the troops, all we got were telegrams and telephone messages saying that the railways were being sabotaged. . . .

From A. Kerensky, *The Kerensky Memoirs*, Cassell & Co., 1966.

E The Cossacks fail to help

The hours of the night dragged on painfully. From everywhere we expected reinforcements, but none appeared. There were endless telephone negotiations with the Cossack regiments. Under various excuses the Cossacks stubbornly stuck to their barracks, asserting all the time that 'everything would be cleared up' within fifteen or twenty minutes and that they would then 'begin to saddle their horses'. . . . Meanwhile the night hours passed. . . . Not a word from the Cossacks . . .

From A. Kerensky, *The Catastrophe*, Appleton & Co. (NY), 1927.

F Red Guardsmen

Red Guards and soldiers who had crossed over to the side of the revolutionaries stand outside the Smolny.

Questions

1 Why were the telephone exchange, telegraph agency and state bank the first targets of the revolutionaries?

2 Why did the Bolsheviks pay particular attention to the railway stations?

3 Is there anything in Trotsky's accounts which helps to explain why the troops expected by Kerensky never arrived?

4 Can you suggest any reasons why the Cossacks decided not to support Kerensky?

5 Explain how you might decide which of the men in the photograph are Red Guards and which army soldiers.

6 Which pieces of evidence in the extracts and the photograph most help to explain why the Bolshevik revolution took place with such little resistance?

28 The revolution completed

By daylight on 7 November the Bolsheviks had taken all the important points in Petrograd. It was time for Kerensky to escape and he describes how he managed this in Source A. Most of the other government ministers who had not been arrested during the night spent the day in the Winter Palace. It was only weakly defended by officer cadets and women soldiers, shown in Source C. However, the Bolsheviks made a great show of capturing the Winter Palace. Sailors who had mutinied brought their battleship, The Aurora, *into position and guns were fired from the Peter-Paul Fortress (which can be seen on the map, page 34). Most of the shots were only gun-cotton 'blanks'. All this impressed Meriel Buchanan who describes the fall of the Winter Palace in Source B.*

A Kerensky describes his flight

We entered my car. . . . Finally we moved. We followed closely all the details of my daily travel through the city. I occupied my usual seat – on the right in the rear. I wore my customary semi-military uniform, which had become so familiar to the population and to the troops . . . I need hardly say that the entire street – pedestrians and soldiers – recognised me immediately. The soldiers straightened up, as they would ordinarily have done. I saluted, as usual. In all probability, the moment after I passed not one of them could account to himself how it was possible for him not only to have permitted this 'counter-revolutionist', this 'enemy of the people' to pass, but also to have saluted him.

From A. Kerensky, *The Catastrophe*, Appleton & Co. (NY), 1927.

B The fall of the Winter Palace

. . . the Ministers, who had sought refuge in the Winter Palace. . . . were guarded only by a company of the Women's Battalion and a few of the cadets from the Military Schools. At six in the evening a message was sent in to them calling on them to surrender immediately, but as no answer was received the attack on the Palace was opened by a few blank rounds being fired from the Fortress* as a preliminary warning. This was followed by a massed onslaught from all sides, armoured cars and machine guns firing at the Palace from under the archway on the square, while now and then the guns of the Fortress or of the cruiser Aurora thundered and crashed above the general din. Actually, however, a good many of the shots were only gun-cotton,* and the firing in all cases was so inaccurate that the Palace was only hit three times from the river.

. . . at about two in the morning the firing ceased and a little later a shouting cheering rabble of soldiers surged across the bridge . . .

Both the women soldiers and the cadets had put up a brave defence, but they were greatly outnumbered and when the Bolsheviks gained an entrance . . . the Ministers, gathered in one of the inner rooms, knew that their only hope lay in surrender.

From M. Buchanan, *Dissolution of an Empire*, John Murray, 1932.

* the Peter-Paul fortress, opposite the Winter Palace

* an explosive material like a powerful firework; fired instead of a shell

C The Women's Battalion

Women soldiers on parade outside the Winter Palace

Questions

1 Imagine a dialogue in which a Bolshevik soldier has to explain to one of his leaders how he had let Kerensky pass.

2 Why were the ministers guarded only by women soldiers and a few officer cadets?

3 Is there any real evidence to suggest that there was a hard battle for the Winter Palace?

4 Why do you think 'a massed onslaught' was ordered?

5 Suggest reasons why the photograph was considered particularly strange when it was seen in Britain not long after 1917.

Part 5

Lenin 1917–1924

29 The one-day parliament

Before the Bolsheviks seized power they had supported a plan to choose Russia's first ever freely elected parliament, the Constituent Assembly. In the elections, the Bolsheviks won only 175 seats compared with 370 for the Socialist Revolutionary Party, which had the votes of most peasants. The Assembly met on 18 January 1918 and the chairman of its first meeting was a Socialist Revolutionary, Victor Chernov.

In this account Chernov describes how the Bolsheviks tried to break up the meeting. Though they accepted the plan for seizing land from the rich and sharing it out, the Bolsheviks did not want the Socialist Revolutionaries to have the credit for it. The SRs, supported by Mensheviks (non-revolutionary socialists) such as Tseretelli, stood firm and the Bolsheviks closed the Assembly by force.

A The Constituent Assembly is closed by the Bolsheviks

When we, the newly elected members of the Constituent Assembly, entered the Tauride Palace, the seat of the Assembly at Petrograd on January 18, 1918, we found that the corridors were full of armed guards. At first they did not address us directly, and only exchanged casual observations to the effect that 'This guy should get a bayonet between his ribs' or 'It wouldn't be bad to put some lead into this one'. . . .

I delivered my inauguration* address making vigorous efforts to keep self-control. Every sentence of my speech was met with outcries, some ironical, others spiteful, often buttressed by the brandishing of guns. . . .

I finished my speech amidst a cross-fire of interruptions and cries. It was now the turn of the Bolshevik speakers. . . . During their delivery our sector was a model of restraint and self-discipline. We maintained a cold dignified silence. The Bolshevik speeches as usual, were shrill, clamorous, provocative and rude, but they could not break the icy silence. . . .

Tseretelli rose to answer the Bolsheviks. They tried to scare him by levelling at him a rifle from the gallery and brandishing a gun in front of his face. . . . Lenin, in the government box, demonstrated his contempt for the Assembly by lounging in his chair and putting on the air of a man who was bored to death. . . .

From V. Chernov, 'Russia's One Day Parliament', *The New Leader*, 31 January 1948.

* opening

When it appeared that we refused to vote the Soviet 'Platform' without discussion the Bolsheviks walked out of the sitting in a body . . . I felt sure we would be arrested. But it was of utmost importance for us to have a chance to say the last word. I declared that the next point on the agenda was the land reform. At this moment somebody pulled at my sleeve.

'You have to finish now. There are orders from the People's Commissar' . . . The lights will be turned out in a minute. And the guards are tired.' . . . leaving the guards no time to collect themselves, I proceeded to read the main paragraphs of the Land Bill, which our party had prepared long ago. But time was running short. Reports and debates had to be omitted. Upon my proposal the Assembly voted six basic points of the bill. It provided that all land was to be turned into common property, with every tiller* possessing equal rights to use it. Amidst incessant shouts: 'That's enough!' 'Stop it now!' 'Clear the hall!' the other points of the bill were voted. . . .

anyone who works on the land

In the dawn of a foggy and murky morning I declared a recess* until noon. . . .

adjournment or break

At noon several members of the Assembly were sent on reconnaissance. They reported that the door of the Tauride Palace was sealed and guarded by a patrol with machine guns. . . . Thus ended Russia's first and last democratic parliament.

Questions

1 In what ways did the Bolsheviks try to intimidate leaders of other parties?

2 What do you think the Bolsheviks most disliked about the Constituent Assembly?

3 Who gave the guards authority to close the Assembly?

4 In your own words, decide what the Land Bill was setting out to do.

5 Imagine a conversation between two peasants who have heard about what happened at this meeting. Would they be pleased or worried for the future?

6 What does Victor Chernov mean by the 'Soviet Platform' which he refused to vote for?

30 The White and Red terror

Very shortly after they came to power, the Bolsheviks began to put pressure on upper-class and middle-class (or bourgeois) people. An example of this was noted in the diary of a Frenchman on the staff of the French ambassador in Russia.

In the countryside the Red Army and Whites (opponents of the Bolsheviks) were acting even more brutally. Source B is taken from the diary of a colonel in a White army. He describes how his men punished a village which had supported the Bolsheviks and where anti-Bolsheviks had been murdered and tortured.

Before these events the Bolshevik Government had already set up the Extra-ordinary Commission against Counter-revolution, Sabotage and Speculation, known everywhere by its short name, the Cheka. *Source C shows how they gave the Extra-ordinary Commission power to carry out an official 'Red Terror' against anyone likely to sympathise with the Whites.*

A The Bolsheviks attack the bourgeois people

Friday 8 February 1918

We are living in a madhouse, and in the last few days there has been an avalanche of decrees. . . . First comes a decree cancelling all banking transactions, then comes another one confiscating houses. A law is being made to take away even their children from the bourgeois: from the age of three they will be brought up in establishments where their parents will always be able to go and see them a certain number of times in the year. In this way, differences in education, which are contrary to the sacred dogma of equality will be avoided, by degrading them all to the same level, that is to say the lowest level of all.

I have made no mention yet of the taxes which continue to hit people from whom all source of income has been removed: five hundred roubles for a servant, five hundred roubles for a bathroom, six hundred roubles for a dog, and as much for a piano.

All inhabitants under the age of fifty are forced to join the 'personal labour corps'. Princess Obolensky has been ordered to go and clear snow off the Fontanka Quay. Others have to sweep the tramlines at night.

From Louis de Robien, *The Diary of a Diplomat in Russia 1917–1918*, Michael Joseph, 1969.

B The White army punish the village of Vladimirovka, 22 March 1918

The head of the column arrived at Vladimirovka about 5.00 p.m. . . . Having surrounded the village they placed the platoon in position, cut off the ford with machine guns, fired a couple of volleys in the direction of the village, and everybody there took to cover. Then the mounted platoon entered the village, met the Bolshevik committee, and put the members to death, after which it demanded the surrender of the murderers and the instigators in the torturing. . . . They were delivered

From M. G. Drozdovsky, *Diary of Colonel Drozdovsky March–April 1918*, Dnevnik (Berlin), 1923; quoted in J. Bunyan and H. H. Fisher, *The Bolshevik Revolution 1917–18*, Stanford University Press, 1934.

to us and executed on the spot. The two officers concealed by the people of Vladimirovka were guides and witnesses. After the execution, the houses of the culprits were burned and the whole male population under forty-five whipped soundly, the whipping being done by the old men. . . . Then the population was ordered to deliver without pay the best cattle, pigs, fowl, forage, and bread for the whole detachment, as well as the best horses.

C The Cheka's decree, September 1918

. . . There must be an end of laxity and weakness . . . A considerable number of hostages must be taken from among the bourgeoisie and the officers. Mass shooting must be applied upon the least attempts at resistance . . . Administrative departments through the militia and the Extraordinary Commission must take all measures to detect and arrest all who hide under foreign names and surnames, with unconditional shooting of all who are involved in White Guard activity. . . .

From W. H. Chamberlin, *The Russian Revolution* Vol. II, Macmillan, 1935

Questions

1 What do you think was the purpose of the decrees described in Source A?

2 What reason was given for taking bourgeois children away from their parents?

3 Can you suggest any reasons why the Whites treated the people of Vladimirovka so brutally?

4 What value would the goods taken from the village be to the Colonel's troops?

5 Does Source B suggest any reasons why the Whites began to lose support as the war went on?

6 Why do you think the Communists put out the order of September 1918 in Source C? What was the purpose of taking hostages?

31 The civil war

The November Revolution gave the Bolsheviks full control only in Petrograd and Moscow. Everywhere else they depended on local groups of Bolsheviks to seize power in each town and village. But in many places they met strong opposition from anti-Bolsheviks. Some were generals and officers of the Tsar's armies. Others were from political groups that the Bolsheviks turned against. All these opponents the Bolsheviks called 'counter-revolutionaries' or 'reactionaries'.

There were also foreign enemies. Until the spring of 1918 the country was at war with Germany. Later there were attacks by Poles, Romanians and Japanese – all hoping to win some land. The centre of the country was held by well-armed Czech soldiers, who had been taken prisoner from the armies of Austria-Hungary. Britain and France sent troops to try to keep Russia in the war against Germany. Some stayed on after the German surrender, in November 1918.

The writer of source A, Arthur Ransome, spent six weeks in Russia in early 1919. He reports what he was told by a Bolshevik official in charge of the all-important railway and road system. Source B shows soldiers from the old army and some Red Guards waiting to sign on for the new Red Army, which the Bolsheviks created to fight the civil war.

A   A Bolshevik describes his work

'Most of our energy at present has to be spent on mending and making railways and roads for the use of the army. Over 11,000 versts* of railway are under construction, and . . . 12,000 versts of highroad. . . . As a matter of fact the internal railway net of Russia is by no means as bad as people make out. By its means, hampered as we are, we have been able to beat the counter-revolutionaries, concentrating our best troops, now here, now there, wherever need may be. Remember that the whole way round our enormous frontiers we are being forced to fight groups of reactionaries supported at first mostly by the Germans, now mostly by yourselves, by the Roumanians, by the Poles, and in some districts by the Germans still. . . . Some of our troops are not yet much good. One day they fight, and the next they think they would rather not. So that our best troops, those in which there are most workmen, have to be flung in all directions. We are at work all the time enabling this to be done, and making new roads to enable it to be done still better. But what waste, when there are so many other things we want to do!

'All the time the needs of war are pressing on us. Today is the first day for two months that we have been able to warm this building. We have been working here in overcoats and fur hats in a temperature below freezing point. Why? Wood was already on its way to us, when we had suddenly to throw troops northwards. Our wood had to be flung out of the wagons, and the Red Army put in its place, and the wagons sent north again. The thing had to be done, and we have had to work as best we could in the cold. Many of my assistants have fallen

From A Ransome, *Six Weeks in Russia in 1919*, G. Allen and Unwin, 1919.

* one verst measures approximately one kilometre

ill. Two only yesterday had to be taken home in a condition something like that of a fit, the result of prolonged sedentary work in unheated rooms. I have lost the use of my right hand for the same reason.' He stretched out his right hand, which he had been keeping in the pocket of his coat. It was an ugly sight, with swollen, immovable fingers, like the roots of a vegetable.

B The creation of the new Red Army

Ex-soldiers and Red Guards wait to sign on in the new Red Army.

Questions

1 Why were railways so important in the Civil War?

2 What does the Bolshevik official consider to be wrong with the Red Army?

3 Suggest reasons why he believes that workmen make the best troops.

4 What does the second paragraph of Source A tell you about the problems of bringing supplies into Moscow? Apart from fuel what other shortage would be really serious?

5 Explain, in your own words, two effects of fuel shortage on the health of people in the office.

6 Can you pick out any figures in the photograph who are likely to be Red Guards rather than ex-soldiers joining up again?

7 Why do you think the Communist government recruited soldiers from the army of pre-Revolutionary times?

32 The New Economic Policy

During the years of the civil war, the Bolshevik government carried out a policy of War Communism. All industry was nationalised and all workers directed to jobs by the state. Even so, the Bolsheviks had difficulty in keeping essential industry and transport going. The biggest problem was the shortage of food for workers and soldiers. Peasants would not supply it when there were no goods to buy in exchange. So food was requisitioned – or seized by armed government officials.

By the end of the war in 1921 there was widespread discontent at War Communism, especially among the peasants. This came to a head when 15,000 sailors at the Kronstadt naval base mutinied. Most were peasants and one of their main demands was for an end to requisitioning. Immediately the mutiny was crushed Lenin declared a New Economic Policy, or NEP. Private trading was allowed and peasants were told that grain requisitioning would end. Instead they would pay a tax in kind – in food goods such as grain. All they had left they could then sell. NEP had two main aims: to increase food supplies and to encourage industry to recover from the war by giving peasants the chance to earn enough cash to buy goods from factories and workshops.

The new policy was announced in March 1921 and this notice appeared in the Communist Newspaper, Pravda, *on 23 March.*

A Announcing NEP

To the Peasants of the Russian Socialist Soviet Republic.
The difficult and destructive war which the Soviet Government carried on for three years with the Tsarist Generals and landlords, with Russian and foreign capitalists ended in the victory of the workers and peasants. In this war, thanks to the heroism of the Red Army, we saved the land of the peasants from seizure by the landlords, did not permit the manufacturers to return to their factories, did not allow the foreign bourgeois countries to deprive Russia of independence or give them her riches to be robbed. The war was very costly and demanded a great many sacrifices from the workers and peasants. Especially difficult for the peasants was the requisitioning of agricultural products, which the Soviet Government was obliged to take in order to feed the many millions of Red Army soldiers, the workers of the railroads and of the most important industrial enterprises. . . .

From now on, by decision of the All-Russian Soviet Central Executive Committee and the Council of People's Commissars, requisitioning is abolished and a tax in kind in agricultural products is introduced in its place.

This tax must be smaller than the requisitions. It must be fixed before the spring planting, so that each peasant may reckon in advance what part of the harvest he must give to the state and what part will remain in his full possession. The tax . . . must fall on the individual household, so that a careful and industrious proprietor will not have to pay for a defaulting fellow-villager. After the tax has been paid the

From W. H. Chamberlin, *The Russian Revolution 1917–21* Vol. II, Macmillan, 1935.

remainder left with the peasant is to be disposed of at his will. He has a right to exchange it for products and machinery which the state will send into the village from abroad and from its own factories; he can use it in exchange for the products which he needs through the cooperatives and through the local markets. . . .

The abolition of grain requisitions and the substitution of a tax in kind will be a great relief for the peasant population and at the same time will strengthen the union of the peasants and workers, on which all the conquests of the Revolution are based. . . .

The time of spring planting is approaching. The All-Russian Soviet Central Executive Committee and the Council of People's Commissars call upon the peasants of Russia to strain all their energy so that not a single desyatin* of arable land will remain untilled. Every peasant now must know and firmly remember that the more land he plants the greater will be the surplus of grain which will remain in his full possession. . . .

approximately one hectare

Long live our valiant Red Army!

Long live the indestructible union of the workers and peasants! . . .

This appeal must be read in all the villages and stanitsas, in factories and Red Army divisons of the RSFSR.

Signed by Kalinin, Lenin, Yenukidze, all the People's Commissars and all members of the Presidium of the All-Russian Central Executive Committee.

Questions

1 What does the notice say were the country's enemies during the Civil War?

2 What reason is given for grain requisitioning during the Civil War?

3 Explain in your own words how the new taxation system was intended to work.

4 What do you think is meant by saying the new system would 'strengthen the union of the peasants and workers' in the fourth paragraph?

5 What encouragement does this notice give to peasants?

6 Why would it be necessary to have the appeal read in so many different places?

Part 6

The Stalin revolution

33 The General Secretary

Lenin died in 1924. By then Stalin was General Secretary of the Communist Party which put him in the strongest position to follow Lenin as the real ruler of the Soviet Union. Yet Source A, from Lenin's political will, suggests that Stalin was unsuitable. In fact it was Lenin's other comrades who were removed from power – and usually executed – on Stalin's orders. This put Stalin in a position to rewrite history as if he had always been Lenin's closest comrade, as the propaganda painting in Source B suggests. Source C is a description by the Yugoslav communist, Milovan Djilas, who visited Stalin in 1944. Source D is a memory of the day of Stalin's death by the poet Yevtushenko who later became known for his criticisms of Stalin.

A Lenin's political will

Stalin is too rude and this fault . . . becomes unbearable in the office of General Secretary. Therefore I propose to find a way to remove Stalin from that position and appoint to it another man . . . more patient, more loyal, more polite and more attentive to comrades . . .

B Lenin and Stalin in 1917 *A propaganda painting made in 1937 showing Lenin and Stalin together at the time of the Bolshevik Revolution. In fact Stalin kept in the background in the Revolution.*

C Djilas visits Stalin, 1944

Stalin was in a marshal's uniform and soft boots, without any medals except a gold star – the Order of Hero of the Soviet Union; on the left side of his breast. In his stance there was nothing artificial . . . this was not the majestic Stalin of the photographs or the newsreels. He was not quiet for a moment. He toyed with his pipe, which bore the white dot of the English firm Dunhill . . . and he kept turning his head this way and that while he fidgetted in his seat.

I was also surprised at something else; he was of very small stature and ungainly build. His torso was short and narrow, while his legs and arms were too long. His left arm and shoulder seemed rather stiff. He had quite a large paunch and his hair was sparse, though his scalp was not completely bald. His face was white, with ruddy cheeks . . . so characteristic of those who sat long in offices. . . . His teeth were black and irregular, turned inward. Not even his moustache was thick or firm. Still the head was not a bad one, it had something of the common people, the peasants, the father of a great family about it – with those yellow eyes and a mixture of sternness and mischief.

I was also surprised at his accent. One could tell he was not a Russian.

From M. Djilas, *Conversations with Stalin*, Hart-Davis, 1962.

D Yevtushenko mourned – at first – for Stalin

On 5 March 1953, an event took place which shattered Russia – the death of Stalin. I found it almost impossible to imagine him dead, so much had he been an indispensable part of life.

A sort of general paralysis came over the country. Trained to believe that Stalin was taking care of everyone, people were lost and bewildered without him. The whole of Russia wept. So did I. We wept sincerely with grief and perhaps also with fear for the future.

From Y. Yevtushenko, *A Precocious Autobiography*, Penguin, 1965.

Questions

1 Lenin was obviously worried about something more than Stalin's bad manners. For what reasons do you thing he suggested that someone else be made General Secretary?

2 What do you think the artist is suggesting about the relationship between Lenin and Stalin in the painting?

3 What do you think the men facing Lenin and Stalin are meant to represent?

4 Why would it be important for Stalin to claim he was close to Lenin in 1917?

5 Pick out three things about Stalin which surprised Djilas.

6 Does Djilas' description suggest any reasons why many Soviet people might have been ready to trust Stalin?

7 What does Source D tell you about Stalin's style of leadership?

34 Against the kolkhoz

Maurice Hindus was born in a Russian village but later became an American citizen. In 1929 he returned to his village in central Russia. That was the year in which Stalin ordered all peasants to join collective farms and pool their fields, equipment and labour. Here, Maurice Hindus describes a visit to the home of Yekim Lavrentin where the talk turns to the peasants' dislike of the collective farm – or kolkhoz.

A Fears about the kolkhoz

The huge coarse table was laden with cucumbers, bread, empty wooden dishes, spoons, round which flocks of flies buzzed viciously. His wife came in with a pail of fresh milk. She strained it into two earthen jars, one of which she set on the table. . . . A poor man this Yekim was, but butter and milk he had in greater abundance than any man that I knew in Moscow . . .

Neighbours had begun to gather. They had heard of my arrival, and they stepped in on their way home from the fields, sickles on their shoulders wooden water-buckets on their backs. They were bursting with eagerness, to talk – and their chief topic was the Kolkhoz.

'There was a time, my dear,' began Lukyan who had been a blacksmith . . . 'when we were neighbours. Now we are bedniaks,* seredniaks,** Kulaks,*** I am a seredniak, Boris here is a bedniak, and Nisko is a Kulak and we are supposed to have a class war. . . .'

'But it is other things that worry us . . . whoever heard of such a thing – to give up our land and our cows and our horses and our tools and our farm buildings, to work all the time and divide everything with others? Nowadays members of the same family get in each other's way and quarrel and fight, and here we, strangers, are supposed to be like one family. Can we – dull-witted muzhiks* – make it 'go' without scratching each other's faces, pulling each other's hair or hurling stones at one another? . . .'

'We won't even be sure,' someone else continued the lament, 'of having enough bread to eat. Now, however poor we may be, we have our own rye and our own potatoes and our own cucumbers and our own milk. We know we won't starve.

'But in the Kolkhoz, no more potatoes of our own, no more anything of our own. Everything will be rationed out by orders; we shall be like mere batraks* on the landlord's estates in the old days. Serfdom** – that is what it is – and who wants to be a serf?'

'Yes, and some women will have ten children and will get milk for all of them; another will have only one child and will get milk for only one, and both will be doing the same work. Where is the justice? Ha!'

From M. Hindus, *Red Bread*, Jonathan Cape, 1934.

* *very poor peasant*
** *a middle (in wealth) peasant*
*** *rich peasant*

* *a peasant*

* *Russian for 'serfs'*
** *before 1861 peasants had been serfs, the property of their lords*

B Working on a collective farm

Red Army soldiers ready to help workers on a collective farm, 1934.

Questions

1 What Communist scheme is Lukyan objecting to?

2 Why does he think it will not work?

3 What reasons do the others have for objecting?

4 Look at the last paragraph. Do you think there is justice in the scheme?

5 List the evidence in the sources which suggests that agriculture was backward by western standards of the time.

6 What would the tools in Source B have been used for?

7 Why might the soldiers have been sent to this farm?

35 For the kolkhoz

While Maurice Hindus was listening to the peasants' complaints against the kolkhoz (see Source 34) a Communist Party official came in. He was not from the village and had the job of organising the peasants into a kolkhoz. Here he argues strongly in favour of collective farming.

Not long afterwards the village began to be planned like the one in the diagram. This shows a successful collective farm. In fact most collective farms never got services such as hospitals or kindergartens.

A The Communist view of the kolkhoz

'I suppose they have been shedding tears about the Kolkhoz,' he said. . . .

'Tell me, you wretched people, what hope is there for you if you remain on individual pieces of land? Think and don't interrupt. . . . From year to year as you increase in population you divide and subdivide your strips of land. You cannot even use machinery on your land because no machine man ever made could stand the rough ridges that the strip system creates. You will have to work in your own old way and stew in your old misery. Don't you see that under your present system there is nothing ahead of you but ruin and starvation? . . .'

'You accuse us of making false promises. Let us see. And please do not interrupt and do not giggle . . . last year you got a schoolhouse; and have you forgotten how we of the Party and of the Soviet* had to squeeze out of you through the voluntary tax your share of the cost of the schoolhouse? And now? Aren't you glad your children can attend school? . . . Were we wrong when we urged you to build a fire station? Were we wrong when we urged you to lay decent bridges across your stream in the swamp? Were we wrong when we threatened to fine you if you didn't take home two loads of peat to mix with the bedding for your stock so as to have good fertiliser for your fields? . . .'

'The Kolkhoz is different,' shouted the old man . . .

'Of course it is different. If we didn't believe in making things different, we never would have overthrown the Czar and the capitalists and the pomieshtchiks.* . . . Different? of course; but better. Don't you see? Isn't it about time you stopped thinking each one for himself and for his own piggish hide? You Kulaks of course will never become reconciled to a new order. You love to fatten on other people's blood. But we know how to deal with you. We'll wipe you off the face of the earth.'

From M. Hindus, *Red Bread*, Jonathan Cape, 1934.

* the local council

* Russian for landowner

B A collective farm *A plan of a later, successful collective farm in the Ukraine in the 1950s.*

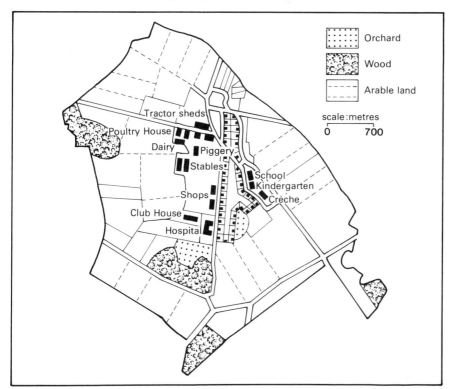

Legend:
- Orchard
- Wood
- Arable land

scale: metres
0   700

Labels on plan: Tractor sheds, Poultry House, Dairy, Piggery, Stables, School, Kindergarten, Shops, Crèche, Club House, Hospital

Questions

1 What practical reasons does the Party official give for a kolkhoz?

2 What other examples of Party activity does the official give in his argument for the kolkhoz?

3 What picture does the passage give of the sort of person who became a Communist Party official?

4 What does the passage tell you of the relationship between the Party official and the peasants?

5 There is no evidence in the passage that the old man threatened in the last paragraph is really a kulak or rich peasant. Why do you think opponents of the collectives were often labelled 'kulaks' by Party officials?

6 Look carefully at the plan (Source B)
a How does it differ from the plan of a village where peasants owned separate farms?
b Using the plans and Source A to help you, describe in your own words how a collective farm worked.
c Is there any evidence in the plan that both men and women worked on the farm?

71

36 The kulak

In this account Maurice Hindus describes the fate of one kulak. Before the Communists seized power many kulaks, like the man in the extract, struggled to build up a living from a time of great poverty and misfortune.

In 1930 the Party leadership ordered an all-out attack on the kulaks, including the confiscation of all their property and their removal from their home districts. Many ended up in labour camps; others were settled in lands where farming was almost impossible. Some who suffered in these ways were not kulaks at all. Others were people, like this man, whose skill and experience could have been of value on the collective farms.

A The fate of the kulak

His first three children died and left him and his wife desolate. The fourth, a girl, grew up well, married and was now living with her husband in a village near. A fifth child, this son of his, Nikolai, came next. They were poor but happy. Now they at least had children and an heir and something vital to live for. But luck was against him. One misfortune after another visited him, his horse died, a fire destroyed his house and barns and burned four grown pigs to death. Left with one toothless old cow he began working for others by the day and saving every copeck* he was earning. When he had five roubles** he bought two calves and fed them on the milk of the old cow, and again misfortune struck him – both calves and the cow died. By that time his Nikolai had reached the age when he could be hired out as a shepherd, and a neighbouring village engaged his services for the summer, paying him twenty pounds of rye for each head of cattle he pastured.

Then the Revolution came, nearby a sovhoz* was started and there he worked on his spare days. With the few roubles he got together he bought from a peasant an old wool-carding machine, and then his real troubles began.

Well, he set the machine to work and in the winter he earned one hundred and fifty roubles. With this money he bought two cows, raised a third, and bought two horses.

Then the Kolkhoz movement reached his village and troubles came to him. Happy with his family on his own land, he saw no reason for scrapping his individualistic household, joining a Kolkhoz and losing his independence.

Soviet officials reprimanded him for his attitude. . . . They levied a tax of one hundred and fifty roubles on his wool-carding machine, and in addition imposed three hundred poods* of rye as his share of the grain collection. He could not possibly meet such an exorbitant obligation. He protested that he never had raised in any one year as much rye as he was supposed to sell to the government. But the officials would not listen. . . . One evening a group of brigadiers came, showed him a paper and said that he was to be 'de Kulakized' . . . and

From M. Hindus, *Red Bread*, Jonathan Cape, 1934.

* *a small coin, one hundredth of a rouble*
** *bank notes*

* *a government-owned farm*

* *about 4800 kilograms*

72

proceeded to confiscate his possessions – cows, horses, sheep, geese, wagons, grain, wool-carding machine, potatoes – everything, and also told him to be ready by next morning to start for the north. . . .

'I tell you it was a nightmare our journey. We were packed into a teploushka* like cattle and there were so many of us . . . And when we got there we were herded into camps without any accommodation – and children died.'

railway van

B A peasant farmer   *A peasant farmer before collectivisation.*

Questions

1 How and when did this peasant start to build up enough wealth to become a kulak?

2 What is meant by an 'individualistic household' (fourth paragraph)?

3 Does the fact that the Communists taxed the kulak mean they were against machinery? What other reasons could there be for the tax?

4 How did the Soviet officials try to 'persuade' the peasant to join a kolkhoz?

5 Why do you think the Communists were against kulaks?

6 From your readings of sources 34, 35 and 36 do you gain any impression of Maurice Hindus's attitude towards collective farms? Give reasons for your answer.

7 Does the photograph suggest any reason why the Communists were so eager to set up collectives?

37 A prosperous collective in 1947

This account of a day spent on a collective farm 80 kilometres north of Moscow is by the American Ambassador to the USSR at the time. Obviously, as this was on official visit, he was shown a well-run and prosperous farm. Yet it was run in the way that all collectives were organised until the 1960s when often several single village collectives were joined into single large units. Modern Soviet farmers receive most of their payment as a monthly wage although they still receive a bonus based on 'work days'.

A Official visit to a collective farm

Its total land area is 1,151 acres, of which 477 acres were in cultivation· On it lived 370 men, women and children in eighty-four households. . . . The total labour force was two hundred adult farmers of working age, sixty-five per cent of whom were women. This labour force is divided into four 'brigades' – a vegetable brigade, two field brigades, and a live-stock brigade. Mr Bakaikin said with obvious grief that of the 110 people who had gone into the Red Army from this collective farm village, forty-one of them had not returned.

[The village] consisted of about twenty-five houses, of from one to three rooms, along one side of a dirt road. The typical impressively large Russian village church now used as a schoolroom and for storage, stood at one end of the village street. In front of the church was the little village store which, in size and construction was very much like a Midwestern American small-town hot dog stand. Each house was surrounded by its own vegetable garden of about an acre. Of the eighty-four households, fifty-five owned a 'private' cow and about forty-five owned one or more hogs. Most of them had a few chickens. In addition the farm itself owned sixty head of cattle, forty-five horses, thirty hogs, and sixty sheep. . . .

In 1946, he said, the farm had produced seventy metric tons of wheat and a fixed percentage, amounting in this case to nineteen metric tons, was sold to the government at the fixed government price. Payment then had to be made in kind to the machine tractor station, which did the tractor ploughing as well as the threshing, and this amounted to seven metric tons. The farm committee had decided to set aside fifteen tons for seed, three tons for the crop insurance fund, two tons for the children's nursery, and to sell another two tons to pay for other production requirements. This left a little more than half of the wheat crop for distribution among the collective farmers, each of whom received grain on the basis of the total number of 'work days' earned during the year.

From W. Beddell Smith, *Moscow Mission*, Heinemann, 1950.

An average farmer, man or woman, was credited with a 'work day' for each day of actual work. Children, who helped with the animals and poultry, were credited with less, usually half a 'work day' for each day's work. Specialists got more, some receiving credit for two, or even three, 'work days' for a day's work.

For each work day, the farmers of Kolos received $4\frac{1}{2}$ pounds [2 kg] of grain, 11 pounds [5 kg] of potatoes, 2 pounds [0.9 kg] of other vegetables, $2\frac{1}{2}$ pounds [1.1 kg] of a straw and $3\frac{1}{2}$ roubles in cash – which was a large income, by Soviet standards.

Questions

1 Work out the numbers of male workers, female workers, children and old people. What was the average size of the household?

2 How much land might each family have owned, on average, if the village was not a collective?

3 Is there any evidence in the passage to suggest that the farm was not truly 'collective'?

4 Why were there so many horses on the farm?

5 The last sentence in the paragraph three seems inaccurate. In what way? Are there other places where the information does not quite add up?

6 What features described in this passage can be found in the plan on page 71?

7 Imagine you are part of a family of two parents and two teenagers. Write an account of a day in your life – the work you and your relatives do, the food you eat, the discussion you have about difficulties in the coming winter.

38 A day in Magnitogorsk, 1933

Part of the plan to industrialise the USSR was to build a huge steel works and a completely new town at Magnitogorsk, once a tiny village in the Ural mountains. For five years, from 1933–38 an American, John Scott, worked there as a welder, since he was sympathetic to the USSR's effort to build up industry. In Source A he describes a day at work and how he and his room-mate, Kolya, spent the evening.

Source B shows the production of some industries at the end of NEP and after the first and second Five Year Plans.

A A day's work at the blast furnace

The big whistle on the power-house sounded a long, deep hollow six o'clock. All over the scattered city-camp of Magnitogorsk, workers rolled out of their beds or bunks and dressed in preparation for their day's work. . . .

From J. Scott, *Behind the Urals*, Houghton Mifflin Co., 1942.

It was January 1933. The temperature was in the neighbourhood of thirty-five below. . . . It was two miles to the blast furnaces, over rough ground. . . .

It was a varied gang, Russians, Ukrainians, Tartars, Mongols, Jews, mostly young and almost all peasants of yesterday . . . Khaibulin, the Tartar, had never seen a staircase, a locomotive, or an electric light until he had come to Magnitogorsk a year before. His ancestors for centuries had raised stock on the flat plains of Kazakhstan. . . . Now Khaibulin was building a blast furnace bigger than any in Europe. . . .

The scaffold was coated with about an inch of ice, like everything else around the furnaces. . . . But besides being slippery, it was very insecure, swung down on wires, without any guys to steady it. It swayed and shook as I walked on it. . . . I was just going to start welding when I heard someone, and something swished down past me. It was a rigger who had been working up on the very top. . . . At eleven o'clock a whistle blew and the workers descended from truss and girder, roof and pipe, to go to lunch . . .

The dining-room was jammed full. . . . The waitress brought . . . plates of hot soup. It wasn't bad soup. There was some cabbage in it, traces of potatoes and buckwheat, and an occasional bone. It was hot, that was the main thing. Most of them had eaten all their bread before the soup was gone. . . . One worker complained: 'if they'd only give us more bread. Two hundred grams isn't enough . . .

Their second course . . . consisted of a soup plate filled with potatoes covered with thin gravy and a small piece of meat on top. . . . It was nearly seven o'clock when Kolya got home. . . . We took our books, wrapped in newspaper, and started off for school.

Many people were leaving the barrack; some were going to the cinema, some to the club but . . . most of them . . . were going to school. . . . They created a student body in the Magnitogorsk night schools of 1933 willing to work eight, ten, even twelve hours on the job under the severest conditions, and then come to school at night, sometimes on an empty stomach and sitting on a backless wooden bench, in a room so cold that you could see your breath a yard ahead of you . . . [to] study mathematics for four hours straight.

It was a little after eleven when I got back to Barrack No. 17.

B The Five Year Plans

	1927–8	1932	1937
Coal m. tonnes	35.4	64.3	128.0
Oil m. tonnes	11.7	21.4	28.5
Pig-iron m. tonnes	3.3	6.2	14.5
Steel m. tonnes	4.0	5.9	17.7
Electricity Thousand million kilowatt hrs.	5.0	17.0	36.2
Woollen cloth m. metres	97.0	93.3	108.3

From Alec Nove, *An Economic History of the USSR*, Allen Lane, 1969.

Questions

1 Can you suggest reasons why there were so many people from different Soviet nationalities at Magnitogorsk?

2 Are there any hints in the early part of the passage which suggest why so many workers attended night school?

3 What three things mentioned had the Tartar (an Asian from south Russia), not seen before he came to Magnitogorsk? What else new might he have found there?

4 What problems would there be in organising work by people of so many different nationalities?

5 Imagine a conversation between two peasants who have newly arrived to work at Magnitogorsk. What would they think of their new life?

6 Using Source B, re-arrange the industries in a table which shows their rank order, starting with the one which made the greatest proportionate increase in ten years.

39 Stalingrad: the story of a town

The Russian-born American, Maurice Hindus, looks back over his memories of Stalingrad. He first knew the town in 1923 at the time of the Soviet government's NEP scheme which allowed private trade in food. Later, he saw it grow into a major industrial city during the first three Five Year Plans of 1928–32, 1933–36 and 1937–41. While Maurice Hindus was writing the book, the people of Stalingrad were resisting the forward thrust of Hitler's troops in one of the greatest battles in World War Two.

A Memories of Stalingrad

I first knew Stalingrad, then still Tsaritsyn, in 1923, shortly after the end of the civil war. . . ., Swarms of homeless children darkened the streets, the bazaars, the pier, the railroad stations, the cemeteries . . .

From M. Hindus, *Mother Russia*, Collins, 1944.

Yet even then no city in Russia, not even Kiev or Moscow, boasted more ample or better food. That was the chief reason for the presence of crowds of homeless children. Nowhere else had I seen so much bread, meat, fruit, vegetables, milk, butter, eggs. The immense sand-blown market place teemed with caravans of carts, drawn by ox, horse or camel and loaded with all manner of produce, including beef, pork and mutton – on the hoof. NEP had struck its stride, and trade was booming . . .

. . . the Soviets only a few years later cleansed it of all private enterprise. I revisited the city in those days. Dark and empty were the rows of booths and shops in the bazaar . . . the Soviets took over everything and launched one of the most ambitious projects of their young career – the erection of a monumental tractor plant, one of the largest in the world. . . .

On June 17, 1930, in the midst of the tempestuous campaign for the fulfilment of the initial Plan, the first tractor rolled off the assembly belt of the Stalingrad motor factory. . . .

By the end of 1932 the population of Stalingrad leaped to four hundred thousand. The Second Plan came and passed. The population rose to half a million and, as formerly, was made up of young people from all over the land. The Third Plan arrived. Stalingrad had changed its very visage. It became, as the Russians love to express themselves, 'an industrial giant', one of the mightiest in the country, and 'a citadel of culture'. Shipbuilding, machine-building, the manufacture of highest grade steel and of precision tools, lumber yards – some as mechanised as any in America – slaughterhouses, textile mills, chemical plants, furniture factories, many other industries . . . and, of course, a manufacturer of arms. . . .

Schools by the score sprang into life. Colleges too – in mechanics, in pedagogy, in medicine, in politics, above all in engineering. Theatres were built, as imposing if not as decorative as any in the country – a youth theatre, a summer theatre, a drama theatre, a musical comedy theatre. Housing was neglected, often woefully. Not that new houses were not built. They were – thousands of them – but as everywhere else in Russia the construction was hasty, often faulty. There was no time and no material, not yet, for modern and comfortable housing. Housing could wait, modern plumbing could wait, electrical refrigerators could wait, many another comfort and pleasure, so common in America and now and then mentioned in the Russian press, could wait. But not factories, not blast furnaces, not engines, not guns nor shells. Neither modern plumbing nor refrigerators nor air-conditioned apartments could frighten away and kill the foreign invader, especially the fascist and the Nazi. . . .

Questions

1 Look at Stalingrad's position on the map on page 89. Can you suggest why the old Tsaritsyn had been an important food marketing town?

2 Why do you think there were 'swarms' of homeless children in 1923?

3 Can you explain why a 'tractor plant' rather than a car factory was established at Stalingrad in the first plan? (Sources 36, 37 and 38 may help you answer this question.)

4 Imagine yourself one of the young people who came to Stalingrad to work during the First or Second Plan. What sorts of reasons would have brought you there?

5 Is there any evidence in the passage to back up the Russian view of Stalingrad as a 'citadel of culture'?

6 Can you explain the Russian emphasis on education and theatres at the expense of good housing?

7 Might Maurice Hindus have been more critical if he had not been writing the book during the time when the USSR was leading the struggle against Hitler?

8 List any similarities between this account of the Russian industrial revolution in Stalingrad and the account by John Scott in Source 38.

40 Propaganda and reality

In the 1930s many people in Britain and America felt that the Communists in the USSR had created a classless society. They believed that workers and managers were treated equally and that there was a true welfare state which took care of all needs in times of sickness, old age, childbirth and so on. This belief arose partly from reports brought back by delegations. The delegations were mostly groups of trade unionists and socialists who visited the Soviet Union and were taken to show-piece factories, homes, nurseries and holiday camps. In Chapter 3 of I was a Soviet Worker Andrew Smith remembers what he was told when he was part of an American delegation which visited a factory in 1929. Three years later he returned to the Soviet Union to work as a fitter. In the extracts from Chapters 6 and 11 you can read how far the truth was from the propaganda.

A First impressions – and reality

Chapter 3

We attended what we were told was a meeting of the workers of the plant. Wages, we learned, averaged about 100 roubles per month. . . . In addition, it was said, the worker received sick benefits, free theatre tickets and many other privileges. Mothers were cared for by the State at childbirth. We were particularly delighted with the nurseries, where apparently the children were being wonderfully cared for. 'The worker is the real boss', our interpreters told us. 'There is no foreman. The workers work freely and not because they are driven.'

From A. Smith, *I was a Soviet Worker*, R. Hale & Co., 1937.

As to homes, our guides explained, every worker receives as much room as he needs, according to the size of his family, the minimum being not more than two persons to a room. We were shown so-called workers' homes where everything was as clean and neat as a pin. It was later that I discovered that these were actually the homes of the higher officials of the plant.

Chapter 6

Kuznetsov lived with about 550 others, men and women, in a wooden structure about 800 feet long and fifteen feet wide. The room contained approximately 500 narrow beds, covered with mattresses filled with straw. There were no pillows or blankets.

Some time later I visited a four storey brick structure about three years old but of slipshod construction. In this building lived about 150 families, divided up into groups of fifteen families within one room each. This group of fifteen families used one kitchen and one toilet . . .

Chapter 11

. . . an announcement was made at a department meeting that a delegation was coming on the following day, that we would have to stay on a Subotnik (voluntary labour) in order to clear up and prepare the factory for the visitors. We were to pay attention only to our machines. Above all we were not to talk. This was to be left to the officials.

After the examination of the factory, the delegation was taken to the *stolovaya* (dining room). Here at last was the only reason for which the workers could be thankful on the occasion of the visit of the delegation. . . . No sour bread 'cutlets', no cabbage soup. Instead there was chicken, vegetables, compote and other delicacies never seen before.

One of the delegates, brimming with enthusiasm at the scene, urged the interpreter to ask the nearest worker how much he had paid for the meal. The worker replied, 'two roubles and thirty kopeks'. Without winking an eyelash, the interpreter turned to the delegate and said, 'Thirty kopeks'.

. . . the delegates were taken to the factory nursery, where the 'workers' children are kept. But now I knew who these workers' children were. They were the children of the various rouged and lip-sticked women . . . whom one could see about the factory, the favourites of the directors. . . .

Questions

1 Make a list of the statements about the treatment of Soviet workers given in Chapter 3. Which of these are proved untrue in Chapters 6 and 11?

2 Can you think of any reasons why American or British trade unionists would have been ready to believe what they were told in 1929?

3 Imagine a group of foreign visitors are to come to your school. Work out two sets of instructions. One asks you to give the best impression possible but not to tell lies about the school. The other is intended to send them home with a quite false picture.

41　A political trial, 1937

*Evgenia Ginzburg was a university teacher and a member of the Communist Party.
She was arrested and then tried for espionage and terrorism, under article 58 of
the Constitution of the USSR. One of the charges was that she had been connected
with a plot to kill Kirov, the Secretary of the Leningrad Communist Party, who
had been murdered in 1934. Actually, the murder had been carried out on Stalin's
orders. In truth, Mrs Ginzburg's worst crime had been to keep quiet and not join
in unfair criticisms of the people she worked with. In this passage she describes
her seven minute 'trial', and the verdict, which had been decided beforehand. In
the end she served eighteen years in labour camps and prisons and was not set free
until after Stalin's death.*

A　The trial of Evgenia Ginzburg

Now my hour had come. The military tribunal of the Supreme Court
– three officers and a secretary – sat facing me across the table; I stood
before them, flanked by two guards . . .

'You have read the charge sheet?' the chairman asked in a voice of
unutterable boredom. 'You plead guilty? No! But the evidence shows
. . . Thumbing through the thick file, he muttered: 'Here's witness
Kozlov, for instance. . . .'

'Not Kozlov – Kozlova* a woman. And a despicable woman at that.'
'Kozlova, yes. And there's Dyachenko.'
'Dyakanov . . .'
'Yes. Well they both state . . .'

But what it was they stated the judge was too pressed for time to say.
Breaking off, he asked me:

'Any questions you wish to ask the court?'

'Yes I do. I am accused under section 8 of Article 58. This is a charge
of terrorism. Will you please name the political leader on whose life you
believe I made an attempt?'

Taken aback by the preposterous form of my question, the judges
said nothing. They looked in reproachful silence at the tiresomely
inquisitive woman who was holding up their work. At last, the grey-
haired one mumbled:

'Don't you know that Comrade Kirov was killed in Leningrad?'

'Yes. But it wasn't I who killed him, it was someone called Nikolayev. And I've never been in Leningrad in my life. Isn't that what is
known as an alibi?'

'Are you a lawyer or something?' snapped the judge. 'No I'm a
teacher.' 'Then don't split hairs. All right, you've never been to Leningrad. But he was killed by people who shared your ideas, so you share
the moral and criminal responsibility.'

'The court will withdraw for consultation', grunted the chairman and
all the performers of the ritual stood up and wearily stretched their
limbs.

From E. Ginzburg, *Into
the Whirlwind*, Penguin,
1967.

*only women's names end
in 'a'*

82

I looked at the clock again. They couldn't even have had time for a cigarette: within two minutes they were back in their seats, the chairman with a large sheet of paper in his hand. It was good thick paper covered with a closely typed and neatly laid out text. The typing must have taken at least twenty minutes. This was the verdict . . .

'. . . To ten years maximum isolation in prison, with loss of civil rights for five years . . .'

Ten years! The air grew light and warm. Ten years! That meant Life!

Questions

1 In what ways does the passage suggest that the court was not very interested in the case?

2 What evidence is there to suggest that the court was not used to accused persons pleading not guilty?

3 In your own words explain the chairman's argument that Evgenia Ginzburg was guilty of terrorism.

4 Pick out any words and phrases in the passage which suggest that the verdict had been decided before the trial.

5 What sentence do you think Evgenia Ginzburg was expecting?

42 A Siberian labour camp

Evgenia Ginzburg spent eighteen years in different labour camps from 1937 to 1955. She was just one of the millions of political prisoners sent to the camps in Stalin's lifetime. Most camps were in the parts of the Soviet Union with the least population and an almost unbearable climate. The prisoners were used to clear land and build railways or canals. Here, Evgenia Ginzburg describes one of her worst times, felling trees in Kolyma camp in eastern Siberia. She and Galya, another political prisoner, were supervised by a camp official, Kostik, who has shown them a tree to be cut down – but they manage only eighteen per cent of the job!

In many other places the work of clearing and building was done by people, especially peasants, who had been forced out of their homes or farms. Sometimes they were supported by volunteers, who were mostly young people from the cities. The men and boys in the photograph were building the Ferghana Canal in the extreme south of the USSR in 1939.

A Living in the labour camp

For three days Galya and I struggled to achieve the impossible. . . . Half-dead ourselves, and completely unskilled, we were in no condition to tackle them. The axe would slip and send showers of chips in our faces. We sawed feverishly, jerkily, mentally accusing each other of clumsiness but we knew we couldn't afford the luxury of a quarrel. The most terrifying moment was when the battered tree began to sway and we had no idea which way it would fall. Once Galya got a hard blow on the head, but the medical orderly refused to put iodine on the wound, remarking:

'That's an old trick. You'd like to be put off work from the start.'

When Kostik came with his yard-stick to measure our daily output, a rifleman stood behind watching him, so even if he had wished to show some compassion it would not have been possible.

'Eighteen per cent – that's all today's output' he would say gloomily, with a sidelong glance at his escort. Then he would write down the figures against our names.

After receiving the scrap of bread which corresponded to our performance, we were led out next day literally staggering from weakness to our place of work. We divided the scrap into two parts. One we ate in the morning with boiling water, the other we ate in the forest, sprinkled with snow. . . .

'Galya, don't you think a snow sandwich is much more satisfying than dry bread?'

'Of course it is.'

During the first day of our starvation diet this sort of nonsense helped to keep up our spirits and to remind us that we were human beings. Before long we were in no mood for joking . . . not only was food related to the fulfilment of the day's norm, which practically all politicals* were too weak to achieve, but failure to fulfil it was treated as sabotage and those who had failed were confined to the punishment-cell.

From E. Ginzburg, *Into the Whirlwind*, Penguin, 1967.

* *political prisoners, not criminals*

This was a shack resembling a public lavatory. We were not allowed out of it to attend to our natural needs and no bucket was provided. At night we had to take turns sitting on the three logs that served as bunks, so most of the time we had to sleep standing up. At about 8 p.m. we were driven there, wet and hungry, straight from the forest, and were marched back to the forest at 5 a.m.

B   Building the Ferghana Canal

Workers from a canal being cut in 1939. The canal, finished in 1950, linked a series of oases in southern USSR. Today sub-tropical crops, mostly cotton, are grown along the area it irrigates.

Questions

1 Explain the system by which rations were given out.

2 Is there any evidence to suggest that the supervisor would have liked to be lenient with the two women?

3 What would you have found the hardest part of camp life?

4 Why did Evgenia and Galya find it impossible to achieve their task?

5 Is there anything to show that the workers in the photograph were probably not political prisoners?

6 What do you think the line of workers are doing in the foreground of the photograph?

7 What does the picture suggest about the level of industrialisation in the Soviet Union by 1939?

Part 7

The Great Patriotic War

43 The German advance

In 1939, at the outset of World War Two, the Soviet Union and Germany were allies. Then suddenly, on 22 June 1941, the Germans invaded the USSR. The political leader in charge of the western districts of the Soviet Union was Nikita Khrushchev whose headquarters were at Kiev. In this extract he describes events from the first German attack in June until the end of the year. By then the invaders had reached the positions shown on the map on page 89.

From 1955 to 1964 Nikita Khrushchev was leader of the Soviet Union. One of the steps he used to climb to power was to attack the records of the two leaders who had gone before him: Joseph Stalin who died in 1953 and Georgi Malenkov who was dismissed in 1955.

A Germany invades the USSR

When the enemy first launched the invasion, we received orders from Moscow not to shoot back. Our leaders issued this strange command because they thought that possibly the artillery fire was a provocation on the part of some German field commander acting independently of Hitler. In other words, Stalin was so afraid of war that even when the Germans tried to take us by surprise and wipe out our resistance, Stalin convinced himself that Hitler would keep his word and wouldn't really attack us.

But within hours our troops met the German invaders in battle and repulsed their first strike. By daylight we got word from the Military District headquarters that German planes were approaching Kiev. Soon they were over the city, bombing the airfield. Fires broke out in the hangars, but fortunately there were no planes there at the time. All our planes had been concentrated along the border under camouflage nets. Our air force, tanks, artillery, and ammunition depots were largely unscathed by the enemy's first strike.

The situation quickly turned very bad, mostly because there was so little help forthcoming from Moscow. Shortly after the war started, during the German advance on Kiev, there was a great wakening of patriotism among the people. The workers from the 'Lenin forge' and other factories around Kiev came . . . in droves asking for rifles so that they could fight back against the invaders. I phoned Moscow to arrange for a shipment of weapons with which to arm these citizens who wanted

From N. Khrushchev, *Khrushchev Remembers*, Andre Deutsch, 1971.

to join the front in support of Red Power. The only person I could get through to was Malenkov.

'Tell me', I said, 'where can we get rifles? We've got factory workers here who want to join the ranks of the Red Army to fight the Germans and we don't have anything to arm them with.'

'You'd better give up any thought of getting rifles from us. The rifles in the civil defence organisation here have all been sent to Leningrad.'

'Then what are we supposed to fight with?'

'I don't know – pikes, swords, homemade weapons, anything you can make in your own factories.'

'You mean we should fight tanks with spears?'

'You'll have to do the best you can. You can make fire bombs out of bottles of gasoline or kerosene and throw them at the tanks. . . .

The Germans moved swiftly into the Ukraine, BeloRussia and Russian Federation. Their occupation of the Ukraine deprived us of our mining and agricultural heartland. We lost the European part of the Soviet Union where our industry was concentrated. A large proportion of our automative production fell into enemy hands when the Germans moved into our industrial base around Moscow. . . .

We were forced to evacuate our industry. Our people, particularly our engineers and technicians, undertook the mammoth task of moving our manufacturing equipment out of the enemy's reach.

Questions

1 For what reason does Khrushchev say the Russian troops were at first ordered not to fight back when the 'enemy first launched the invasion'? Can you suggest any other reasons why such a command was given?

2 According to Khrushchev, for what reason did the situation 'quickly turn very bad'?

3 How much use would rifles have been in the defence of Kiev?

4 How did Malenkov react to Khrushchev's request for weapons from Moscow?

5 Why was it so important for the Soviet Union to move their industry out of German reach?

6 With what kind of reputation does Khrushchev emerge from this extract?

7 Do you have any reason to doubt Khrushchev's interpretation of the events?

8 Use the map of page 89 to calculate the distance advanced by the Germans between June and December 1941. What was the average advance per day? What problems did the advance bring for the Germans? Did it bring any advantages to the Soviet Union?

44 The siege of Leningrad

The map illustrates the main events in the war from 1939 to 1942. In 1939 and 1940 the Soviet Union took land to the west with the agreement of Hitler. On 21 June 1941 the Germans turned on the Soviet Union and advanced nearly to Moscow by December. A Soviet counter-attack towards Smolensk (see Source 45) pushed them back safely from the Soviet capital. In 1942 a further German advance took the Germans to the outskirts of Leningrad by February and to Stalingrad by November. There followed the great battle for Stalingrad described in Sources 46 and 47. Meanwhile Leningrad was holding out in a twenty-eight month siege which was not lifted until June 1944.

The Communist official in charge of Leningrad during the siege was Andrei Zdhanov. The story in Source A is taken from a Russian book based on diaries kept by Leningraders during the siege.

A   The effects of the siege

One day Zdhanov called in General Mikhail Dukhanov. He had received a report of a dangerous outbreak of dysentery among youngsters in a boarding school. With typical bureaucratic suspicion he thought the school administration might be stealing food and depriving the children.

Dukhanov appeared at the school shortly after daybreak, hoping to catch the thieves at work. He watched the food checked out of the storehouse and into the kitchen, watched it cooked and examined the inventory. All was in order.

He stood by as the children ate breakfast – 25 grams and a mug of hot water with salt. . . .

For lunch they had 50 grams of bread and a pat of butter, a little soup made of frozen beets and some cereal which seemed to be mostly linseed-oil cake. General Dukhanov noticed that many children put part of their cereal and soup into jars. He thought that they were saving it to eat later on. But he was mistaken. Soon those who were able to walk appeared in heavy clothes. They were going home to visit their relatives. Most of them clutched a glass or jar in which they were carrying food for a starving mother, brother or sister. General Dukhanov wanted to halt the youngsters and speak to them. But he suddenly realised that there was nothing to say. He went back that evening and reported to Zdhanov that there was no stealing, just lack of food.

He asked Zdhanov if he had been right not to stop the children as they were leaving the school.

Zdhanov spoke slowly: 'I would have done the same thing.'

Then he turned and took up the telephone: 'This is Zdhanov speaking. Within forty minutes put down a heavy barrage on the Nazi regiments of Majors Grudin and Witte. What for? In order to inflict heavy casualties on the fascists.'

From H. Salisbury, *The Siege of Leningrad*, Secker & Warburg, 1967.

B The German advance into the USSR

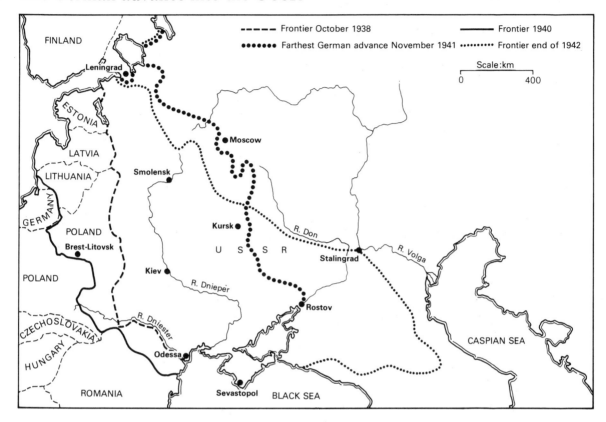

Questions

1 List the lands taken by the USSR in 1939 and 1940. Does the map suggest any reasons why they should have done this?

2 Use the map to explain the importance of the Soviet counter-attack in the winter of 1941–2.

3 Does the map suggest any reasons why the Germans moved south-east in their 1942 campaign? Do you know of any other reasons?

4 How much bread do you estimate there is in 25 and 50 grams?

5 Why do you think General Dukhanov 'realised that there was nothing to say' to the children?

6 What is the writer suggesting as Zdhanov's reason for ordering the guns to fire at the Germans?

7 Look at the position of Leningrad on the map. Does it explain why the Germans were never able to take Leningrad?

45 The effects of war

From June to December 1941 the Germans pushed into Soviet territory to the outskirts of Moscow. Then the Russians launched a winter counter-offensive to save their capital. One of these counter-attacks took the Red Army through Dorogobuzh, a village about 80 km east of Smolensk (see the map on page 89).

Alexander Werth, a Russian-speaking journalist, travelled with the Soviet forces. Here he describes what the German invasion had meant to the people of Dorogobuzh and some nearby towns and villages. The sufferings of these people were actually not yet over, for the Germans later re-occupied this district.

A Suffering caused by the invasion

The town of Dorogobuzh . . . had been bombed by the Germans, and now nothing was left of it but the shells of the stone and brick buildings and the chimney stacks of the wooden houses; of its 10,000 inhabitants only about 100 people were still there. In July, in broad daylight, waves of German planes had dropped high explosives and incendiary bombs over the town for a whole hour. There were no troops there at the time: men, women, children had been killed – nobody knew how many.

After spending the night in an army tent outside the town . . . we drove to Yelnya through what was now 'reconquered territory'. There had been heavy fighting there. The woods were shattered by shellfire; there were here and there large mass-graves with crudely painted wooden obelisks* on top of them, in which hundreds of Russian soldiers had been buried. The village of Uchahovo, where some of the heaviest fighting had taken place for over a month, had been razed to the ground and only from the bare patches along the road could one roughly imagine where the houses had stood. In Ustinovki, another village some distance away, most of the thatched roofs had been torn away by bomb blast, the people in the village had fled before the Germans came but now there were faint signs of life again. An old peasant and two little boys had returned since the Russians had recaptured the village, and were working in deserted fields, digging up potatoes that had been sown before the Germans had come. And there was nobody else in the village, except an old woman, a blind old woman who had gone insane. She was there when the village was shelled and had gone mad. I saw her wandering barefooted about the village carrying a few dirty rags, a rusty pail and a tattered sheepskin. . . . she just stared with her blind white eyes and never uttered any articulate words, except the word *Cherti* – the devils.

We drove on to Yelnya, through more miles of uncut fields. . . . Yelnya had been wholly destroyed. On both sides of the road leading to the centre of the town, all of the houses – mostly wooden houses – had been burned, and all that was left was piles of ashes and chimney-stacks with fire places some way down. It had been a town of about 15,000 inhabitants. The only building still intact was a large stone

From A. Werth, *Russia at War*, Barrie & Rochcliffe, 1964.

* pyramid shapes

church. . . . The town had been captured by the Germans almost by surprise and very few civilians had had time to escape. Nearly all the able-bodied men and women had been formed into forced-labour battalions and driven into the German rear. A few hundred elderly people and children had been allowed to stay on in the town. The night the Germans decided to pull out of Yelnya – for the Russians were closing in, threatening to encircle, the town – the remaining people of Yelnya were ordered to assemble inside the church. They spent a night of terror. Through the high windows of the church black smoke was pouring in, and they could see the flames. For the Germans were now going round the houses, picking up what few valuables they could find and then systematically setting fire to every house in the town. The Russians drove into the town through the burning wreckage and were able to rescue the now homeless prisoners.

Questions

1 What had happened to the town of Dorogobuzh?

2 Explain what is meant by 'reconquered territory'?

3 Explain in your own words how the civilian people of this district had been affected by the war.

4 How do you think events such as those described here affected Soviet food supplies during the war? Give reasons for your answer.

5 What were forced labour battalions?

6 What effect do you think events such as these would have had on the Russian people's determination to carry on with the war?

46 A German lieutenant's diary

In the summer of 1942 the Germans crossed the River Don on their way to the Volga (see map on page 89). But their advance was halted at Stalingrad by the bravery of Russian soldiers who resisted street by street. Some of the fiercest fighting took place round a grain elevator and the Barrikady factory, actually on the banks of the Volga. Once the Germans had struggled this far, the Red Army was able to bottle them up in Stalingrad with huge numbers of planes, tanks and heavy guns. The German General von Manstein could not break through the Russians to help the Germans and they were forced to surrender. After the battle Soviet soldiers found this diary on the body of a German lieutenant.

A From the Don to Stalingrad

August 2 What great spaces the Soviets occupy, what rich fields there are to be had here after the war's over.

August 23 Splendid news – north of Stalingrad our troops have reached the Volga and captured part of the city.

September 8 The Russians are defending themselves with insane stubbornness.

September 11 Wherever you look is fire and flames . . . Russian cannon and machine guns are firing out of the city. Fanatics.

September 13 The Russians are fighting desperately like wild beasts, don't give themselves up but come up close and then throw grenades.

September 16 Our battalion plus tanks is attacking the elevator from which smoke is spouting – the grain in it is burning; the Russians seem to have set fire to it themselves. Barbarism. The battalion is suffering heavy losses. . . . The elevator is occupied not by men but by devils that no fires or bullets can destroy.

September 20 The battle for the elevator is still going on.

September 22 Russian resistance in the elevator has been broken. Our troops are advancing towards the Volga. We found about 40 Russian dead in the elevator building. Half of them were wearing naval uniform.

September 28 Together with our tank crews we have taken the south part of the city and reached the Volga. We paid dearly for our victory. In three weeks we have occupied about $5\frac{1}{2}$ square miles.

October 4 Our regiment is attacking the Barrikady settlement. A lot of Russian tommy-gunners have appeared. Where are they bringing them from?

October 10th The Russians are so close to us that our planes cannot bomb them.

October 27 Our troops have captured the whole of the Barrikady factory but we cannot break through to the Volga. The Russian artillery on the other side of the Volga won't let you lift your head.

November 10 A letter from Elsa today. Everyone expects us home for Christmas.

From V. Chuikov, *The Beginning of the Road,* McGibbon & Kee, 1963.

November 21 The Russians have gone over to the offensive on the whole front. . . . Then, there it is – the Volga, victory and home to our families! We shall obviously be seeing them next in the other world.

November 29 We are encircled.

December 3 We are on hunger rations.

December 18 General Manstein is approaching Stalingrad from the south with strong forces.

December 25 The Russian radio has announced the defeat of Manstein. Ahead of us is death or captivity.

December 26 The soldiers look like corpses or lunatics, looking for something to put in their mouths. A curse on this war.

B The liberation of Stalingrad

A Russian soldier waves a victory flag over a ruined square in Stalingrad, February 1943. The last German HQ was in the building partly covered by the flag.

Questions

1 Describe, in your own words, the changing attitude of the lieutenant to the Russians and to the war.

2 Which words and phrases give you clues about the lieutenant's opinion of the Russians?

3 Why do you think the Germans bothered to attack the grain elevator? Why did the Russians set fire to it?

4 Can you suggest any reasons why the lieutenant thought it worth noting that there were sailors in the elevator?

5 Why could German planes not help the soldiers on 10 October?

6 Can you suggest why the diary entries are mostly short towards the end?

7 How does the photograph support the evidence in the diary about the street fighting?

Postscript

47 Khrushchev's attack on Stalin's record

Nikita Khrushchev was an important Communist official from the 1930s. After Stalin's death in 1953 he became First Secretary of the Party and in 1955 he used this position to make himself the most powerful man in the Soviet Union. In February 1956 he spoke for three hours to hundreds of Communists from all parts of the Soviet Union who were meeting for the Party's Twentieth Congress. He praised Lenin's leadership and sharply attacked the cruelty of Stalin's rule. He went on to accuse Stalin of encouraging his own glorification by the 'cult of the individual', even to the extent of rewriting his own biography.

In the 1930s the Russian security police was known as the NKVD, which for a time was headed by Yezhov. Later Beria was put in charge of 'the organs of state security'. By the time of Khrushchev's speech, Beria had been executed and the military section of the Supreme Court (which dealt with offences against the state) was busy declaring the innocence of many thousands who had been sentenced to death or labour camps. This was known as 'rehabilitation'.

Krushchev's speech is often called the 'secret speech' because it was made to a session of the Congress which was not reported in the press. Some copies, however, passed round the USSR and one or two reached the West.

A The 'secret speech'

Stalin's wilfulness against the Party and its Central Committee became fully evident after the 17th Party congress which took place in 1934. It has been established that of the 139 members and candidates who were elected at the 17th Congress, 98 persons i.e. 70 per cent, were arrested and shot, mostly in 1937–8. (Indignation in the hall.) The same fate met not only the Central Committee members but also the majority of delegates to the 17th Party Congress. Of 1,966 delegates . . . 1,108 persons were arrested. . . .

The vicious practice was condoned of having the NKVD prepare lists of persons whose cases were under the jurisdiction of the military Section of the Supreme Court and whose sentences were prepared in advance. Yezhov would send these lists to Stalin personally for his approval of the proposed punishment. In 1937–8, 383 such lists containing the names of many thousands of Party, Soviet, Komsomol, Army and economic workers were sent to Stalin. He approved these lists. A large part of these cases being reviewed now and a great part of them are being voided because they were baseless and falsified. Suffice it to say that from 1954 to the present time the military section

From The Observer, 1956.

of the Supreme Court has rehabilitated 7,679 persons, many of whom were rehabilitated posthumously. . . .

When Stalin said that one or another should be arrested, it was necessary to accept on faith that he was an 'enemy of the people'. Meanwhile, Beria's gang, which ran the organs of state security, outdid itself in proving the guilt of the arrested. . . . And what proof was offered? The confessions of the arrested, and the investigating judges accepted these 'confessions'! And how is it possible that a person confesses to crimes which he has not committed? Only in one way – because of the use of physical methods of pressuring him, torturing. . . .

Comrades! The cult of the individual acquired such monstrous size because Stalin himself, using all conceivable methods, supported the glorification of his own person. One of the most characteristic examples of Stalin's self-glorification and his lack of even elementary modesty is in the edition of his *Short Biography* which was published in 1948. . . . We need not give here examples of the loathsome worship filling this book. All we need to add is that they all were approved and edited by Stalin personally and some of them were added in his own handwriting to the draft text of the book.

Writes Stalin:

Stalin's military mastership was displayed both in defence and offence. Comrade Stalin's genius enabled him to divine the enemy's plans and defeat them. The battles in which Stalin directed the Soviet armies are brilliant examples of operational military skill.

Comrades! We must abolish the cult of the individual decisively, once and for all.

Questions

1 What does Khrushchev state to be the worst years of Stalin's terror?

2 Why should there have been 'indignation in the hall' at the death of the 98 people who were members or candidates (i.e. junior members) of the Central Committee when hundreds of thousands of others died?

3 What examples does Khrushchev give of Stalin having a personal hand in the terror?

4 Why did people confess to being enemies of the people?

5 What example does Khrushchev give of the 'cult of the individual'? Why should this be seen as a particularly evil thing in the Soviet Union?

6 Why do you think Khrushchev made this speech at a secret session of the Party rather than at a public meeting or on the radio?

Acknowledgements

We are grateful to the following for permission to reproduce copyright material:

Andre Deutsch Ltd and Little Brown and Co. Inc. for an extract from *Khrushchev Remembers* edit./trans. Strobe Talbott, © 1970 Little Brown and Co. Inc.; author's agents on behalf of the Estate of Meriel Buchanan for extracts from *Dissolution of an Empire*; Jonathan Cape Ltd for extracts from *Red Bread* by Maurice Hindus 1934; The Century Co. for extracts from *Documents of Russian History 1914–1917* by Golder 1927; Collins Publishers Ltd and Harcourt Brace Jovanovich Inc. for an extract from *Into the Whirlwind* by Eugenia Ginsburg; Granada Publishing Ltd for an extract from *The Beginning of the Road* by V. Chiukov, McGibbon and Kee 1963; William Heinemann Ltd and Harper and Row Inc. for an extract from *Moscow Mission* by W. Beddell Smith; author' agents for an extract from *Mother Russia* by Maurice Hindus; Macmillan London and Basingstoke for extracts from *The Russian Revolution*, Vol. II by W. H. Chamberlain, 1935; *The New Leader* for an extract from the article 'Russia's One Day Parliament' by V. Chernov *The New Leader* 31.1.48, Copyright © The American Labor Conference on International Affairs Inc.

We have unfortunately been unable to trace the copyright holders of extracts from *My Life* by L. Trotsky, *Russia at War* by A. Werth, and *Memoirs of Lenin* by N. Krupskaya, and would appreciate information which would enable us to do so.

We are grateful to the following for permission to reproduce photographs: BBC Hulton Picture Library, pages 4, 9, 15, 21, 27, 28, 31, 39, 41, 57; Novosti Press Agency, cover and pages 11, 17, 45, 47, 55, 73, 85, 93; Pathe-Cinema, page 63; Popperfoto, page 66; Society for Cultural Relations with the USSR, page 69.